Married to the Shepherd

Vikki Simmons

CREATION
HOUSE PRESS
A STRANG COMPANY

MARRIED TO THE SHEPHERD by Vikki Simmons
Published by Creation House Press
A Strang Company
600 Rinehart Road
Lake Mary, Florida 32746
www.creationhouse.com

Unless otherwise noted, all Scripture quotations are from the King James Version of the Bible.

Scripture quotations marked NIV are from the Holy Bible, New International Version. Copyright © 1973, 1978, 1984, International Bible Society. Used by permission.

Word definitions marked *Strong's* are the author's interpretation of the definitions from *Strong's Exhaustive Concordance of the Bible*, ed. James Strong (Nashville, TN: Thomas Nelson Publishers, 1997).

Word definitions marked *Thayer's* are the author's interpretation of the definitions from Joseph Thayer, *Thayer's Greek-English Lexicon* (Peabody, MA: Hendrickson Publishers, 1996).

Cover design by Terry Clifton

Library of Congress Control Number: 2004107760
International Standard Book Number: 1-59185-618-3

04 05 06 07 08— 987654321
Printed in the United States of America

To J. D., my precious husband, my pastor, father of my children, and my best friend. Outside of Jesus, you have made my life so happy and complete on this earth. Thank you for loving me like Christ loved the church, for we are truly "one flesh," and I will always treasure you as my most precious gift from God. (IWFLYYHOMY)

Contents

Foreword

A FEW YEARS AGO I spoke at a women's conference on the topic, "Help! I'm a Pastor's Wife." I opened my heart and shared experiences and lessons that I had learned along the way as a copastor and pastor's wife. Since that time I have talked and prayed with many pastor's wives. Whether she is the wife of the senior pastor, youth pastor, or halfway between, the cry is the same: "Help! I'm lonely, not prepared, incapable, hurting…" And the list goes on! Yes, it is true, as a pastor's wife you may have "many afflictions" or misunderstandings and hurts, but as the Word says, "He truly delivers us from them all."

You will certainly feel the heartbeat of my friend, Vikki Simmons, as she shares some of her life experiences as the shepherd's wife. Her heartfelt desire is for every pastor's wife to come into her own relationship with God and into a place of security and confidence knowing that God has not only called the "shepherd" but the "shepherdess" as well.

I am excited about Vikki's writing this much-needed book…just for the shepherd's wife. Read it prayerfully with an openness to receive the Word of the Lord to you personally. Allow the Holy Spirit to minister to you as you learn to walk boldly in all that God has for you, and as Vikki says, "It is possible to be the Shepherd's wife and be better…not bitter."

—ROSELLA RIDINGS
PASTOR'S WIFE AND COPASTOR
ORLANDO, FLORIDA

Chapter 1

The Beginnings

"VIKKI, LET'S NAME her Vikki." That was the scene on that hot August day in 1951, in the crowded maternity ward of Fayette County Memorial Hospital. My mother and father were signing the birth certificate before leaving the hospital and taking their newborn daughter home. My parents were not giving me an unusual name, but a popular name with a different spelling. They had seen the spelling of my new given name in a local newspaper that had written an article highlighting the life of the popular singer, Vikki Carr.

Neither my mother nor my father was really interested in the meanings of names. It was only the sound of the name that prompted them to call their 8½ pound, dark, curly-headed girl Vikki, with two K's.

I am sure that when my wonderful parents, Jack and Jean Souther, held me and gazed into my deep blue eyes, they never considered the destiny that my heavenly Father had already planned for my life. He knew my life from beginning to end, and He had chartered a course that was going to be adventurous, to say the least!

There would be many difficult and unknown places and experiences. And some of those experiences would afford me great pain and hurt. But if I allowed the Lord to keep me on course, my life would be filled with His contentment. That contentment would be not unlike a calm, picturesque sea lying below a glimmering sun shining down in peaceful and restful warmth. The peace of the Lord would be my blanket.

The course that my heavenly Father had mapped for me was given with such precision and detail. Because of His life, I was given "abundant life" provided through His Son. And what is abundant life? Here is my definition: *abundant life* is the privilege of reflecting the image of Jesus in my life. And if I would live in that abundant life, I would be able to reflect His glory to those who surrounded me. For the abundant life was not so much for my benefit as it was for others to see Him. I would be sent in that abundant life to peoples and places, carrying His glory, and revealing His love while simply being *married to the shepherd.*

ENTERING

Now, you might have thought that the title to this first chapter should have been named *the beginning.* That seems to be the most likely name. For I am aware, just as you are, that we all have a beginning. In reality, our entire life is full of beginnings!

Everyone has many beginnings. Every minister's wife who reads this book will have many beginnings and endings in her life. That will be a constant on which she can depend! Dr. Edwin Cole wrote in his book, *Entering and Leaving Crisis,* that each one of us has, from before our birth until our death, a life filled with beginnings and endings that we enter and leave. And that, he calls *crisis.*

You see, it was a crisis that we entered into when we were born. When we left infancy to enter adolescence, it was crisis. Trying to learn to walk was a major crisis as a toddler because we experienced many falls. The good side of that time in our life is that the majority of us do not remember trying to learn to walk. So the pain of those falls is mostly nonexistent in our conscious minds.

We then left adolescence to enter our teen years. That was a crisis. Then we left our teen years to enter young adulthood—being out on our own, making our own decisions, thinking that our parents were not very smart and definitely ill informed. That was certainly a major crisis.

Then we left being single and entered into marriage. This is when our parents became the most intelligent people on the face of the earth. We not only left the single life and entered marriage, but also entered the life of being married to a minister. And you talk about *crisis!*

As for me, after two years of marriage with no children, I entered the world of the great adventure of parenting. Now that was crisis! And for some of you, you may still be in that crisis, and your children are now fifty years old!

This leads us to leaving the world of a home with children and entering the empty nest syndrome. But do not get too comfortable here. They come back!

I guess the greatest crisis to date is when we leave the world where our bodies are full of the vigor of youth and vitality and enter the world of menopause. Should we call that time of our life a major crisis?

It is a fact that all of these segments, put together, spell out our life. And each segment consists of an entering and a leaving with crisis.

Now, you will see in this book that I love to study words. Because, to me, words seem to possess this great drama of scene after scene of hidden mysteries. That may sound kind of strange, but the words we hear and say most often have more than just one dull meaning. And when you and I begin to study the words of our heavenly Father and our Savior, Jesus Christ, those scenes bring with them such an ostentatious portrait of real life dressed with an indescribable beauty.

So let's begin this journey by first looking at the word *crisis*. When I looked up possible synonyms for the word *crisis*, I found these:

- emergency
- dilemma
- urgency
- turning point

I do not know about you, but in my life, all of these words are fitfully suited together to describe the different phases of my life. So, will you agree, all of us have beginnings? And if you agree, you will know that those beginnings and endings can and will chart the course of your life. It will help you to also know how we leave one phase will determine how we enter another.

In other words, if you were loved and caressed as an infant, most likely you will carry a sense of love and security through your adolescent years. If you were neglected as a child, then you could possibly carry rejection and insecurity into all the other entering and leaving stages of your life.

One of the benefits in finding Jesus as our personal Savior

is that we have secured the sure answer to victory over rejection and insecurity, for He is truly the only one who can deliver our hearts from the torment of neglect.

The prophet Isaiah told us that He was "despised and rejected by men; a man of sorrows and acquainted with grief" (Isa. 53:3). And because He knows and understands more about rejection and grief than you and I will ever know, we can come to Him and receive exactly what we need in order to secure our victory!

It is most likely that you and I will collect a lot of what we term *baggage* in life, when, in reality, most of it is garbage. And sometimes we allow that garbage to set and pile up. And you know what happens to garbage when it sits around for a while! It begins to have this rank odor. And how do we deal with smelly garbage? We throw it out! We do not try to cover it up with a delightful smelling deodorizer. Otherwise, it will not be long before the odor will simply overcome the perfume. Cover-up will not destroy the horrendous odor of neglect. It will simply do what it says it will do—cover up.

In the case of rejection and neglect, those seeds were most likely sown when we were children, so we cannot just cover them up and pretend like they do not exist. We have to get rid of them by giving them to our Savior. He is the only one who can carry that burden.

Can I give a side bar right here? I pray that the Holy Spirit will right now give you a *rhema* word of revelation in the importance of finding Jesus, as a child. To me, the most important workers in our churches are the nursery workers and the children's church workers. They have the greatest mission. For if our children find Jesus while they are young, their entering and leaving stages of life will be crises filled with the opportunity to allow the Word of God to give them great victories that they would not otherwise experience!

Do you know what a *rhema* word is? Let's look at what the apostle Paul said to the church at Rome. In Romans 10:17 the Word of God says, "So then faith cometh by hearing, and hearing by the word (*rhema*—the spoken word) of God." The word *word* here is *rhema* and it means "a word uttered by a living voice; spoken with understanding" (Strong's). Let me illustrate this to you by using my youngest daughter, Andrea.

Andrea was a very social child, and she loved being around people. But what we did not know, until she went to college, was that she had attention deficit disorder. Her personality had carried her through the elementary and high school years of her life with little or no interruptions. But she needed more than personality when it came to completing her college level material.

When the psychologist interviewed her, he told her that she was highly intelligent. He said that her IQ was very high and that she would have no problem being a doctor or lawyer, if that is what she wanted to pursue. The only problem was that her attention span was very short, so she could not focus on one certain thing for any length of time.

When she was in high school, I remember how I would get her attention concerning cleaning her room. For the majority of our ministry, I had to work at some job full time. When Andrea was around fifteen years old, I would get ready to leave for work, telling her, "Andrea, clean your room before you leave for school. We are having company over tonight and you won't have time to do it when you get home from basketball practice." She would look at me and say, "No problem, Mom. Consider it done!"

I would return home from work before she came home from school, and I would walk past her bedroom door, looking in, only to see massive devastation! Surely someone or something had come to an end in that room!

When Andrea would come home, I would say to her, "Now Andrea, you did not clean your room." She would look straight at me and say, "I'm so sorry, Mom. I forgot." For some reason, I believed her. She was not very good at hiding a lying face. I genuinely believed that she did not disobey me on purpose, for I had this keen discernment that she was telling the truth—at least this time. So, I knew that I had to take another approach in order for her to retain any important thing that I was going to say to her.

The next time that I needed for her to do something and retain my words in her memory, this is what I did. I would take my hands and put one on each side of her face and look straight into her eyes. I would make sure that she was looking into my eyes and I would repeat these words very slowly and methodically: "ANDREA...CLEAN...YOUR...ROOM... BEFORE...YOU...GO...TO...SCHOOL!" Then, I would make her shake her head with my hands still on her cheeks so that she fully understood. That gave her a reference point to remember my words when she looked at her room. And when I returned home on those occasions, her room was cleaned because she had received a *rhema* word!

All through this book the Holy Spirit is going to place His hands on your face and look straight into your spirit and give you a *rhema* word. And if you receive those words, the entering and leaving stages of your life in ministry will begin to have a meaning of fullness and completion.

ENTERING: OUR FIRST FLOCK

Let's start with the *leaving crisis* of single life to the *entering crisis* of being married to a shepherd (a minister). Allow me to give you my story. And for the sake of time, I am going to give it to you in a bullet-point form.

- Saved at the age of seven, but had no biblical training on how to apply the Word of God to my everyday life, even as a child.

- Started playing the piano at the age of four and became the major pianist in adult church at the age of eleven.

- Preached my first sermon at twelve years old to my younger cousins at Grandma's house. My text was from Luke, chapter 18, concerning the rich man and Lazarus. I preached on hellfire and brimstone. (Maybe that is why no one wanted to stay in the room!)

- Raised as a teenager to go to church. My father was a good moral man, and he became a Christian soon after I married.

- Left for college at eighteen. Met J. D. the first day of school.

- Engaged in two weeks. Married in four months. Married on Sunday afternoon and started working at a church as associate pastor and music director on Wednesday.

- Raised a "Liberal Yankee" and married a "Conservative Rebel."

- Went to work at a large, old, established church in the South where there was no family or friends for miles.

- Lived in the basement of the fellowship hall, in a Sunday school room that had been turned into a bedroom, with a sink and tin shower connecting with the room.

- No experience as a wife and certainly no experience as a minister's wife. In all sincerity, I was eighteen years old going on twelve, but I was so happy to start my new life!

Now let me enlighten you on some of the things that J. D. and I experienced in the short nine months of ministry at our first church. J. D. was hired as associated pastor/youth pastor. He also worked from 6:00 a.m. to 2:30 p.m. five days a week at a local furniture factory. I was hired as music director of the church and taught piano lessons in the afternoons.

Here is what our neighborhood was like:

- The local "bootlegger" lived directly across from the church and our place of residence.

- Next to his house was the home of the prostitutes.

- Next to that house lived a murderer that had been released from prison not too long before J. D. and I moved across the street. I was awakened one morning to the noise of police sirens and saw a man lying in the grass with his chest split open. He had gotten into a fight and was seriously injured.

I am sure you are saying to yourself that you wished that you had such an exciting beginning. Allow me to continue this intriguing saga. The church was quite the friendly church. Two families in the church did not speak to each other and had not for years. They attended church every Sunday but they sat on opposite sides of the church. (I truly think that they had forgotten what had made them angry with each other.)

The pastor's wife and some of the women decided to take me as their main project for shaping and molding into the ideal minister's wife. What a job!

I changed my outward appearance to long-sleeve, middle-of-the-calf, black, brown, navy, and maroon polyester, non-form fitting, homemade clothing. I let my hair grow long again, and what little makeup I wore came off. No jewelry, except for my new wedding band, was allowed. No, this was not 1920! It was 1970.

Along with my outward appearance changing, my countenance began to change, too, in trying to conform to the "rules" of dress. I see now that that should never dictate our spirituality or bring bondage about in our hearts. We should only enter a place of submission in dress or behavior so that we can minister the Word of God to those who truly have deep convictions concerning their appearance and spirituality, for there are sincere, loving Christians who have convictions concerning their appearance. We, as ministers, must be sensitive to that for the reason of reaching them.

The apostle Paul said in Romans 14:13:

> Let us not therefore judge one another any more: but judge this rather, that no man put a stumblingblock or an occasion to fall in his brother's way.

He continued to say:

> If your brother is distressed because of what you eat, you are no longer acting in love. Do not by your eating

destroy your brother for whom Christ died.
—ROMANS 14:15, NIV

A great deal of the people in that church believed that certain outward appearances dictated your spirituality. And if I fought against them and their conviction, they would never have been able to receive the Word of God from me or see the love of Jesus in my heart toward them. Without the reality of the love of Christ operating in my life, they might not have ever been able to overcome any bondage that comes with legalism.

The confusion and hurt that I was experiencing inwardly was not the dress code but was the double standard that I saw concerning loving one another. It came from those whose heart was cold toward the things of God and the delusion that you did not have to show love toward each other.

It was not just the rift with the two families. The young people were the wildest bunch that I had ever seen. They were not allowed to attend "worldly places" like bowling, football games, or skating. The external limits were set for them, and that is OK. But the condition of their hearts, which were full of carnality, was never dealt with.

The youth choir was asked to sing at the state camp meeting, and without my knowledge, two of the boys were drunk while singing during the service. When my husband confronted the parents, their response was, "Well, boys will be boys."

Because they had won the state competition, they were sent to St. Louis, Missouri, for the national competition. Now, this was a first and a last for me. Some of the girls brought their Polaroid cameras and took self-portraits while showering and gave the pictures to the boys. Then on the way home…well, let me just say, "Never again!"

When we arrived home and stepped off of the bus J. D. said, "Honey, we've got to go back to college and hopefully get some education to help us in the ministry." I thought we were getting plenty of education. But, back to school we went—and what a relief!

So, this was the story of experiencing "our first flock." I am sure some of you have a more dramatic or, you may call it, "tragic" beginning. But what is most important in our beginnings as ministers of the glorious gospel is that we must be convinced of two things. If you and I receive a *rhema* word concerning these two things, then everything concerning our purpose in life, while being married to the shepherd, will fall into place. I consider these two things most important in the life of a shepherd's wife. They are very simple, yet so profound.

The first thing that we must know is this: what does God really think about you? And the second is that you and I must know that He will always be there!

WHAT DOES GOD THINK ABOUT YOU?

It is so easy for us to look in the Scriptures and see what the Father God thought about His Son, Jesus. We know that He loved Him. But let's look at what God thinks about you and me.

In Jeremiah 29:11 the Lord is speaking to us:

> For I know the thoughts that I think toward you, saith the LORD, thoughts of peace, and not of evil, to give you an expected end.

The New International Version says:

"For I know the plans I have for you," declares the LORD, "plans to prosper you and not to harm you, plans to give you hope and a future."

The psalmist wrote in Psalm 139:17–18 (NIV):

How [which is an exclamation like the word *wow*] precious to me are your thoughts, O God! How vast is the sum of them! Were I to count them, they would outnumber the grains of sand. When I awake, I am still with you.

So, here it is. God thinks about us all the time. And His thoughts about us are *precious*, which means they are "highly valued; costly; esteemed very valuable and very rare," which makes them precious (Thayer's).

They are not only precious, but they are numerous. That means there would be no possible way that a man could even begin to count them and get a number, unless he could count the grains of sand on the earth. And the number of thoughts would be greater.

My husband and I have lived near a coastline for about twenty of the thirty-four years of our marriage. We love the ocean and like to take walks on the beach. Many evenings in those twenty years we would wait until sunset and ride to the beach and walk in the darkness with either the moon or the stars as our light.

Without exception, the Holy Spirit would use the ocean breeze and the tumbling of the waves and the peaceful seclusion of just the two of us to bring our minds back into focus. We would realize how great He really is and how vast His plans are for us. We would leave there refreshed more times than not.

I would bend down and take a handful of sand and remember Psalm 139:18. I thought of the impossibility of counting the grains of sand that I held in my hand, let alone all the sands of the sea, or the sands of the desert or the sand that covered the entire earth. And yet, the Lord says that His thoughts toward us are more numerous than the sand. (See Psalm 40:5.)

The Lord is not just talking about these three places. He is also referring to the addition of all the sand at the bottom of the ocean, all the different types of sediment in molten volcanic rock, all other vast rock formations that cover the earth, even down to the sand that may be in your backyard.

In actuality, it would be adding all the sand over the entire earth. And still the Word of the Lord to us is this: "His thoughts toward us are more numerable!" (Psalm 40:5, author's paraphrase). And this is our assurance. His thoughts are all good and not evil. They are thoughts that we will experience in a future, with a hope filled with Him.

Here is the brilliant deduction of it all. If you have thoughts that are not good, but evil, where do you think they originate? Could they possibly come from the enemy of your soul who has absolutely no good thoughts about you at all?

The psalmist goes on to write in Psalm 40:5:

> Many, O LORD my God, are thy wonderful works which thou hast done, and thy thoughts which are to us-ward: they cannot be reckoned up in order unto thee: if I would declare and speak of them, they are more than can be numbered.

The reason they cannot be numbered is because they are all in the vastness of God Almighty. They are constant and such a part of Jehovah that they cannot be arranged or put in order to count them!

The psalmist just says that they are so vast that even while I am sleeping and I am so unaware that He is thinking about me, God has thoughts about my future, and they are peace and hope! And when I wake up and become aware of my surroundings, He is still having thoughts of me! And they are never evil, but always good!

What are some of the thoughts that you would like God to have concerning you? Do any of them relate to fulfilling your needs and insufficiencies? Are you hoping that the thoughts about you are thoughts of help from heaven?

Here are some of the thoughts that I believe God is thinking about you:

- He loves how He made you so different. He created no other person just like you. No one has your exact DNA. You are uniquely special.

- He loves all the gifts and talents He put inside of you. And He thinks about how He can use them so the world will see Him!

- He loves your hair so much that He has given every one of them a number. And being a hairdresser, I know that it is normal to lose between seventy and eighty hairs a day. Each one of those hairs is added to the count, so that your heavenly Father knows from before you were born to date how many hairs you have had on your head. How awesome!

- Because you are born again, every time He looks at you, He sees you through the blood of His Son, Jesus. And you know how much He loves His Son!

- He wants you healthy. He put an immune system within you that will ward off certain diseases without any assistance from medication. And then when you needed more, He allowed mankind to acquire knowledge to help in the area of medicine. And when their knowledge goes as far as it can go, His thoughts and actions come in a magnitude of ways that will reveal that He is your Healer.

- He wants to prosper you. One way to make prosperity and health come to you is "as your soul prospers" (3 John 1:2).

- His plans are set and ordered for you. And God takes delight in every one of them. (See Psalm 37:23.)

- He thinks about you loving Him with a pure love. He even provides the means by which that love can happen because He went ahead and "smeared" His love in your heart by His Holy Spirit. (See Romans 5:5.)

- He already has planned all of your escape routes that you could ever need to take when you are tempted. He thinks about how happy you are going to be when you overcome temptation. (See 1 Corinthians 10:13.)

- He knew that you would marry a pastor, and He has good thoughts and plans concerning all the joys that you should, could, and would have in the ministry together.

- He knew that you would have pain, persecution, and rejection. He knew that through Him you would be "more than a conqueror!" You would not just conquer, but you would gain a surprising victory!

These are just a few of the numberless thoughts of good that the Lord has for His children. Now, you know the good thoughts that you have toward your children. Why would you even think that the Lord would be any different toward you?

It is important for us to remember that God is not working on plan B in our life. He is always working with plan A. We cannot surprise Him or stump Him in any way. He orders our steps. He knew us from the foundations of the world. So before we were ever born, He knew our life from the beginning to the end.

Again, He knew that you would marry a minister. He knew the choices that you would face and which ones the devil would try to use to separate you from Him. God's ways and thoughts are higher than ours. (See Isaiah 55:9.) That means that His answers for our most difficult questions and His ways for escape will be out of our scope of natural thinking. God's way is always sure and precise. He will not fail us because He will reveal to us what we are to say or do, as well as what not to do and what not to say.

But the responsibility of obedience falls upon us. We have to be a doer of His Word! (See James 1:22.) If we are a hearer only, we will be tossed around in life, like a volleyball, never knowing whose hands are going to volley us into delusion. The devil will make sure that at some point in our life, we are spiked to the ground, with no help from anyone!

But God is our "very, present help in trouble!" (Ps. 46:1). Even when we are weak and helpless we can just "call upon Him and He will answer. He will be with us in trouble. He will deliver us and honor us. With long life, He will satisfy us and show us His salvation" (Ps. 91:15–16, author's paraphrase). If I did not believe that, I could not trust His good thoughts concerning me. I do not know about you, precious shepherd's wife, but I must trust the Lord in my life, and the life of my family and our ministry. Nothing else is stable. Nothing else is sure but Him.

KNOWING GOD IS NOT GOING TO LEAVE YOU!

Now, you know somewhat the thoughts that God has toward you. But do you ask the question, where is God in relationship to me and my life? Well, here is the simple truth. He is never going to leave you! Even if we think that there has to be more to that answer, we will be mistaken. God is here to stay. This is His promise. In Hebrews 13:5 it says:

> Let your conversation be without covetousness; and be content with such things as ye have: for he hath said, I will never leave thee, nor forsake thee.

It is so simple. With every emotion that you experience, God is there! In every hard task or impossible trial, God is right there with you! When people in your church speak down to you and your husband, God is there, and He hears every word and knows every motive behind every word.

Be assured that He is taking notes and has already judged their attitude. But your response to their attitude is what He is most concerned with, for it is your attitude that you are responsible to take charge of and put in order. How can we fix someone else's attitude if ours is out of control?

It is like looking through the beam in our eye, trying to pick out the speck of sawdust in our brother or sister's eye. We cannot do it because we cannot see clearly. It is almost virtually impossible to see a speck of sawdust even when we have clear vision.

In Matthew 7:3–5 (NIV), Jesus discusses our willingness to conquer our attitudes before we tackle someone else's. He says:

> Why do you look at the speck of sawdust in your broth-
> er's eye and pay no attention to the plank in your own
> eye? How can you say to your brother, 'Let me take the
> speck out of your eye,' when all the time there is a plank
> in your own eye? You hypocrite, first take the plank out
> of your own eye, and then you will see clearly to remove
> the speck from your brother's eye.

Remember, the Lord has not left you during the aggravated times of your life. He is right there with you! He has seen and heard everything. Again, nothing is hidden from His eyes. And because He is not going to leave you or forsake you, He will give you instructions on how to handle your attitude when dealing with the faults of others. The word *forsake* means that He is not going to desert you or "leave you helpless in the matter" (Strong's).

And here is the instruction to you and me concerning oth-
ers. We do not work on them. We work on us! If we reverse His instruction, He labels us "a hypocrite." (See Matthew 7:3–5.) Do you really know what a hypocrite is? Well, the Greek word for *hypocrite* is "an actor; a pretender; a dissem-
bler" (Thayer's). The Lord says that we have a beam in our eye and what the other person has is a "speck of sawdust." And if we try to remove their bad attitude (speck of sawdust) and do not take in consideration the beam (judgmental attitude) in our eye, He calls us a "hypocrite."

I do not know about you, but I do not want to be labeled a hypocrite! Jesus said that the Pharisees were hypocrites and they were the most religious people around. On the outside, they looked flawless, but inside they were only dissemblers of perfection. They were merely acting so others would not see the great darkness within them. But their acting was never hidden from the Lord. He was always there, observing their pretense.

Our goal is to know that because the Lord is always with us, we must be vigilant in being real inside and out, because He does not miss a thing! We cannot hide our feelings and attitudes from Him. They are always exposed in the presence of His righteousness. And the only way to live the abundant life is to make His righteousness our righteousness!

This illustration of the speck and the beam is more on the negative side of the omnipresence of God. Let's look at the positive benefits of the reality of knowing that the Lord will never leave us or forsake us.

In Deuteronomy 31:6 it says:

> Be strong and of a good courage, fear not, nor be afraid of them: for the LORD thy God, he it is that doth go with thee; he will not fail thee, nor forsake thee.

It is here that Moses is beginning his instruction to Joshua concerning his leading Israel over to the Promised Land and overtaking their enemies. Notice that his instruction to Joshua begins with four attitudes within himself that he must portray in his leadership. He must:

- Be strong—which meant that he had to be bold, firm, encouraged, and strengthened. He had to prevail.

- Of good courage—which meant that he had to be alert, brave, determined, and had to exhibit strength and be solid in his convictions.

- Not fear—which simply meant that he could not be afraid, terrified, or in awe of his enemies.

- Not be afraid—which meant that even to the extreme emotions of terror, fear, or dread that he might face, he could not allow himself to break, fear, become oppressed, or tremble because of his enemies.

Now, Joshua knew that he could never do these things within himself. He knew that no human force could help him conquer fear and terror, let alone make him become strong and courageous. Joshua's only help was in God, and that help was in God's going with him and that God was not going to fail him or forsake him!

This is why Joshua was able to be strong and courageous and to not be afraid or fear anything. It was because God went alongside him, leading and moving him to victory. The word *fail* meant that the Lord was not going to relax or slacken when it came to supporting Joshua. He would not withdraw from Joshua at any moment or second of Joshua's life. He was Joshua's "very present help in trouble!"

The word *forsake* meant that God would not depart, loosen, and leave behind, neglect, abandon or desert Joshua. It has the meaning that the Lord would not "turn on" him. He would not leave Joshua to survive on his own. God was going to be the reason for Joshua's courage and strength. There would be no other help but God!

Now, because the Lord is "no respecter of persons" (Acts 10:34), we must apply this instruction of the promise of victory to our own lives, especially in the ministry.

Our heavenly Father is saying to us:

Be strong and of good courage. Do not be afraid of anything or anyone. I, the Lord, will not fail you [not one time], nor will I leave you. I will not forsake you even when you have forsaken Me. I will not turn on you in order to destroy you. I love you and will always be your help! Just trust Me!

—Deuteronomy 32:6

Dear Pastor's wife, you are never alone. Even when you feel alone, the Lord is there to lift you in your loneliness and cause you to feel worth because you are valuable to Him. Your mistakes and failures do not dictate the presence or absence of His mercy, grace, and love toward you. "Surely goodness and mercy is following you all the days of your life" (Ps. 23:6).

If you and I will ever grasp the value and worth that we are to the Lord, we will then begin to receive the revelation that "nothing can separate us from the love of God in Christ Jesus" (Rom. 8:39). For you and me to be strong and courageous, to not fear or be afraid, it takes a revelation deep inside our spirit-man from our heavenly Father.

Pray this prayer with me:

Father, in Jesus' name, by Your Spirit, touch me in my inner being with the revelation that You are always with me, even when I fail. For I must know, O Lord, that my failure will not diminish or dilute Your love toward me. It is when I fail or when I sin that fear comes in, and courage and boldness leave. I repent of all my sin and ask You to cleanse me by the blood of Jesus. Restore, Lord, the confidence of our relationship that comes in my repentance. I need to feel You right now, Father. Touch my heart with Your presence. Hold me, Lord. I thank You for Your faithfulness. I love You!

Chapter 2

Submitting to the Chief Shepherd

Submit yourselves therefore to God. Resist the devil, and he will flee from you.

—JAMES 4:7

COMMIT OR SUBMIT?

OF ALL OF the chapters in this book, I feel this one is the most pivotal. For if we know how to submit to our heavenly Father, then and only then can we truly submit in all other areas of our lives. So how do we submit to God? Is it through commitment? Is there a formula that we can follow? Why is it so difficult, at times, to do?

Every one of us has to find the answer to these questions. As a pastor's wife, how could I ever expect any of my flock to submit to the Lord if I did not? More importantly, what about my children, my family, and my friends? How could they ever see, by my example, that there really is something to this Christian life? Finding the answer would exemplify the difference to them of life being real or life being superficial! For me, it was a must that I found the answers.

So I began to pray and ask the Lord, "How do I submit to you, Father?" To my surprise, His response was quick, tender, and very clear. One thing you and I can count on concerning our heavenly Father is that He will not leave us wandering about like lost sheep. He will answer us with clarity and precision. And there will be no doubt concerning His will in this matter because it affects our entire relationship with Him.

The answer I received from the Lord was also very dramatic. For with the revelation came the awesome conviction that I must submit in order to further my relationship with Him. The Lord knew that I was determined to know Him, so He spoke "loud and clear." And this is what He said to me, "Vikki, submission has only one facet in your life, and that is *surrender*." Now, that was not the answer I was expecting to hear. Surrender. Doesn't that sound final? I heard the word *finality* jumping out to me. And I saw finality as the main characteristic of the word *surrender*, and that frightened me! In my mind two words were standing in line right behind final. And here they are: *give up!*

Then it got worse. I heard the words *relinquish control and become vulnerable*. OK, I have heard enough! But what I did not realize at that moment was that my fear and hesitancy were coming from my fleshly soul. My will, my emotions, my desires, my ambitions, my way, my, my, my was getting in the way of my receiving the blessing of knowing my heavenly Father intimately!

My problem was not my spirit-man. For the Lord Jesus had made my spirit new through the shedding of His blood. My spirit was willing, ready, and jumping up and down with excitement to surrender. But my unregenerate mind and carnal flesh were screaming, "abuse...abuse...abuse!" The good thing is that my mind and my flesh did not have their way. When I realized what was happening, I looked at my problem and found my solution. I did not want to surrender, but I had to surrender!

Now, we as Christians do not fully understand the meaning of *surrender*. Because of that lack of understanding, we are kept from knowing the meaning of how complete and final surrender really is! And to be honest, I believe we need some finality in our lives!

The black and white of life continues to fade in our eyes, and we see more and more gray, which brings to us much insecurity and unhappiness. We never seem to make ourselves happy. Everything that we have to offer ourselves just does not seem to be enough! So we look for another route...an easier way.

And this is what we do. We say and even act like we are surrendering, but in actuality we are doing something much easier. What we have done, as Christians, is we have supplanted the word *surrender* with a more gracious and popular term. The word is *commit* or *commitment*. Commit sounds much more refined, with even a hint of elegance to it. But surrender has the sound of being lowered to the act of slavery and even goes as far as to the point of degradation.

Linguists tell us that when a word becomes popular during an era of society, it normally replaces another word. Sometimes the meaning of the new word changes somewhat in its definition and operation of the former word. In the case of the word *commitment,* it has the meaning of "pledge, promise, duty, and even responsibility." But *surrender,* on the other hand, means "to relinquish, renounce, abandon, or to give up." Commitment does not mean surrender or vice versa.

With commitment you and I can become uncommitted. But when we surrender to something we have to totally let go of our rights, privileges, and desires. That is what we do when we surrender to our Father, God. We give ourselves over to His control, and we relinquish our own will and those things that we want to control.

The fact is that many of our problems stem from our commitment to God instead of our surrendering to God. And know this: many of the problems that you and your husband will deal with in the ministry will come either from your own nonsurrendered life or from your church members who have not surrendered to the will of the Father.

Can I tell you by experience that the majority of my difficulties in the ministry stemmed from my own personal nonsurrender to the Father? Let me explain. I could not stop a lot of the things that bombarded my husband and me in the ministry. Many things that happened were out of our control. Then again, I brought many things upon myself through selfish desires. I thought that I had the answers, while the Holy Spirit was speaking to my heart to do something totally different. But I had to have my way! And my way got me into a lot of trouble and brought to both my husband and me a lot of pain.

So, Who Is Really Our Enemy?

Here is our problem with surrender. You and I have to understand that it is not that we do not surrender. We do surrender, but it is to the wrong persons. I say "persons" because we really have two enemies—the devil and our flesh. Let's look first at our enemy, the devil. He is the first one that we want to accuse, so let's look at who he is and what he does.

First of all the devil, our enemy, is a defeated enemy. That is what the Word of God says about his position in relationship to us. We are fighting a "defeated foe." How do we know that? Well, let's look at two of the many scriptures that prove that the devil is defeated.

In Colossians 2:15 (NIV), the apostle Paul talks about Jesus:

> And having disarmed the powers and authorities, he [Jesus] made a public spectacle of them, triumphing over them by the cross.

Another scripture is found in 1 John 3:8 (NIV):

> He who does what is sinful is of the devil, because the devil has been sinning from the beginning. The reason the Son of God appeared was to destroy the devil's work.

The key words in these scriptures are *disarmed* and *destroy*.

The word that is translated *disarmed* means "having spoiled." It comes from two Greek words that mean "to strip, to put off by separation, to despoil, and disarm" (Strong's).

Here is a simple illustration. If a bomb was active at one time, but someone disarmed it, it would still be called a bomb. It would look like a bomb and have all the same outward characteristics of a bomb. But when it was disarmed, the power to be destructive was removed. It no longer has the resident power within it to blow up, shatter into pieces, or cause annihilation. Why? Because it had been disarmed!

27

The timer can run out. The sound of the click in the trigger device can even be heard. But the power to explode in order to destroy is gone!

Jesus disarmed the devil at the cross for those who would receive Him as Lord. Oh, the devil will still look and act like the destructive villain that he professes to be. He will still try to bring to us the fear of what he can and will do to destroy everything about you and me, or anything that belongs to us. But Jesus says, "I have disabled him for your sake."

Dear shepherd's wife, do not allow the enemy to bring fear to you about what he *appears* to be. Let the Holy Spirit reveal to you what our Savior, Jesus, *caused* him to be. The devil is not only disarmed, but also Jesus said He has destroyed his works for your sake.

The word, *destroy*, in 1 John 3:8, means "to break up; to demolish; to dissolve or to literally make a zero." So Jesus made the devil "a zero." This is why it is so important for you and me to know to whom we are surrendering. Our complete surrender should be to our Victor, Jesus Christ, the Son of the Living God. For it is through Him that we can say that we have victory in our life and our ministry. But remember the victory is experienced in surrender because the responsibility of the victory rests upon the Lord, not upon us. How can we win except we do it His way?

When I received the revelation (that *rhema* word) from the Lord concerning my enemy, the devil, my battle with him and his cohorts changed dramatically. My prayers were full of faith to My heavenly Father. I would recognize, by the Spirit, the enemy's strategic plan to destroy or disassemble my life, my family, my friends, and my church. Sometimes, he would fight against one of these and sometimes he would attack all of them at the same time. But the key was that I knew it was the devil.

The Holy Spirit was so faithful to bring back to my remembrance the Word of God concerning God's battle plan. The scripture that He would always bring to my heart was Ephesians 6:12. He would say to me, "Remember, Vikki, you are not fighting against flesh and blood even though people are the vehicle that the enemy is using as his weapon against you." Then I heard the Lord say, "Your responsibility is to do what my Word says for you to do, and that is obey me!"

According to James, chapter four, I had to "submit and resist." Now, my problem in obedience was that I would want to resist the devil before I would submit to God. But God has an order to follow, and we cannot deviate from His plan.

OUR ENEMY IS HERE, AND IT IS US!

So, who is the other villain in this story? It is our flesh. Now, this enemy has been my most productive enemy. It has been productive because I have many times allowed my flesh to live instead of "crucifying it daily."

You may be asking, "What is the flesh?" The flesh is not the skin or muscle that covers our skeleton that I am referring to here. It is the human nature that we possess, the cravings and desires that we have and everything that is connected to what we want, versus what God wants.

The battle with my flesh seemed so hard for me. I remember questioning the Lord concerning His words, "the spirit indeed is willing, but the flesh is weak" (Matt. 26:41). My response to the Lord was "No, that's not how it is with me, Lord. My spirit is weak, and my flesh is strong. That is why I give in to my flesh. It's just so aggressive, Lord. It's got to do what it wants to do."

But the true revelation came when I began to ask "to know Jesus and the power of His resurrection" (Phil. 3:10). I began to study this scripture and found the meaning for the two words that described our spirit and our flesh. The word *willing*, describing our spirit, means "predisposed." It comes from two Greek words that mean "out front" and "with fierce, strong passion" (Strong's). The word *weak*, which describes my flesh and yours, means "sick, impotent, feeble, weakest, and without strength" (Strong's).

I said, "OK, Lord, why is it, in my case, that it seems to be the very opposite? My spirit seems to be the weakest, and my flesh is so strong because it seems to win out more than my spirit." This is how the Holy Spirit responded to me. He said that our new, born-again spirit is strong, willing, and ready to obey everything that our Lord has commanded us to do. Because of Jesus, our spirit has the power to accomplish the will of God in our lives. But our flesh is so sick, weak, feeble, and without any strength. It constantly shouts out, "I cannot do this. I'm too weak. It's too hard. It hurts." And so, our flesh wins the battle because it just falls down and lies there in front of the will of God and will not budge!

It is like a rebellious child that wants to do something but he has been told, "No!" So that child falls on the floor, limp with dead weight, and screams his head off until the parent gives in. This is what we do with our screaming flesh. It is crying, "No, No, No, No! I don't want to do that!" And just like our discipline for our children has changed from spanking to "time out," we refrain from slapping our flesh and telling it to get in line with God's Word. "Time out" does not work with our flesh. It just regroups and becomes stronger the next time it wants to disobey.

The apostle Paul said that his flesh was so rebellious that he had to "beat it" into submission to the will of God. This is what he said in 1 Corinthians 9:27 (author's paraphrase):

No, I beat my body and make it my slave so that after I
have preached to others, I myself will not be disqualified
for the prize.

What were the disciplinary weapons that the apostle Paul
used? They were prayer and the Word of God.

Jesus told the disciples in the garden, "If you want to overcome temptation, you have to watch and pray" (Matt. 26:41,
author's paraphrase). He told His disciples that they were
going to have to be aware of the surrounding temptations
and then pray. It was His words to them and their knowledge
of Scripture that would renew their minds so that they would
not be ignorant of the devil's devices.

It was Peter who said that we have a "more sure word of
testimony" and that was the "already written Word of God."
Peter was anointed by the Holy Spirit to tell the church that
the Scripture was a "more sure word of prophecy" (2 Pet.
1:19) than their actual physical relationship with Jesus.

You see, Peter had been with Jesus from the beginning of
the Lord's ministry. He had experienced miracles that you and
I long to see, but may never see in our natural lifetime. He
even experienced the glory of God on the mountain and actually saw Moses and Elijah. And yet, he says that the prophecies
of the Word of God given through the inspiration of the Holy
Spirit were greater and of more value than all the miracles
that he experienced in the flesh. How could he say that?

Well, all the miraculous things that he experienced in the
physical did not keep him from denying the Lord. If he had
only obeyed the words of Jesus in the garden, "watch and
pray," he would have had the power to submit to God and not
the temptation. Now you may think that sounds too simple.
But, precious pastor's wife, it has to be simple because we are

dumb sheep. And God knew that He had to make it simple for us in our salvation or we would never know how to receive His salvation through His Son.

Now, do not get offended when I say that you and I are dumb sheep. I know that you may not have ever said it, but you have probably thought it many times: your church is full of stupid sheep. Not stupid because of ignorance, but stupid because of rebellion. If you and I ever expect our sheep to become smart, we had better get smart ourselves! Because we are not only the shepherd's wife, but we are also sheep. There is more said about that in chapter four.

SUBMISSION: ATTENDING THE DAILY CRUCIFIXION

Now, we will experience a result that will bring us pure unhappiness; this will happen when we choose to refuse to crucify the flesh on a daily basis. What happens is that live flesh brings about that pseudo-Christian life, which has at its foundation the absence of obedience to God. Our thinking becomes foolish in that we believe that it is actually possible to resist the devil without submitting to God. It will not work! It is God's way or no way! By surrendering to His way, we really find our life filled with genuine happiness and peace.

So submission comes only through unconditional surrender to our heavenly Father. And when we fully surrender, submission becomes a natural response for us. We lose those destructive mind games that we play with ourselves. You know what they are: *Does God really want me to do this? Is this just my flesh talking? Can I submit some other way? Is it possible to do what the Lord has asked of me in some other fashion?* Total surrender causes those thoughts to fade quickly, and in some cases, never to come to the forefront of our minds. Why? Because it is no longer our daily way of life.

Ask yourself this question: How many times have you thought about leaving your house without first brushing your teeth? I would say very few times, because it is part of your life and mine to brush and floss before we see anyone on the outside. It is your lifestyle. Total surrender brings about a lifestyle of crucifying the flesh daily. Then, and only then, does the abundant life that Jesus promised us rise to the surface.

You are not your own anymore, dear pastor's wife. You have been bought with a price, and it was a great price. But you were worth the price paid by the Father. He gave His only Son so that He could restore His family to Himself.

It has always been about family. God wanted a family, and He paid for it with His Son's blood. And now that you and I and have been restored to His family, it is our number one responsibility to go out and get as many of those lost family members that we can find and bring them to the Father's table.

Here is the true fact of submission. It is only when we submit first to our heavenly Father that we are able to submit to our husbands or to one another with genuine humility. And really, true and genuine humility only comes through surrender. Paul wrote to the church at Ephesus, saying, "Wives, submit yourselves unto your own husbands, as unto the Lord"(Eph. 5:22). Look at the last four words: *as unto the Lord*. Here is the gauge for our submission to our own husbands. Are we submitting to our husbands like we submit to the Lord? This may answer a lot of questions concerning your marriage relationship with your husband.

Are there problems in your marriage? Is the relationship strained between you and your husband? Could it be that you are submitting to your husband like you submit to the Lord? Is it "kind of" but not really? Our submission to the Chief

Shepherd is actually the surrendering of our heart to our heavenly Father. He is the only One to whom we surrender our heart! And we must fully surrender our heart to Him, not partially, without fear of abuse or mistreatment. He will never mistreat us or abuse us. The Lord has to have our whole heart in order to guard every inch of it against someone or something that may try to destroy it!

When we surrender our heart to the Father, His Holy Spirit seals it. Our heart is water proofed, fire proofed, dent proofed, and puncture proofed. Nothing can penetrate it in order to destroy us due to the sweet anointing oil of the Holy Spirit. Everything runs off our heart. Nothing can attach itself to our heart because of that precious oil. This revelation is vital in our life of ministry because the attack from the enemy comes to cause us to believe that he can destroy us.

Abuse may come to kill us. Words of hatred from people in your church, cherished friends, or even family members, may try to penetrate your heart in order to cut you up into pieces so that you are unrecognizable. Precious shepherd's wife, know this: if you are fully surrendered to God, He becomes your responsible Warrior. And remember, nothing can penetrate or destroy Him. For the enemy would have to come through Him first to get to you! And that is never going to happen! Hallelujah! So surrender your heart fully to God. That is the first step. Then you can submit to your husband.

The word *submit* in the Book of Ephesians means "to arrange under, voluntarily." It means "to cooperate or have the spirit of cooperation" (Thayer's).

Paul tells us to "submit to our husbands, as unto the Lord." He is saying to us that our response to submission should be with the same attitude as our surrender to God. We cannot partially submit. We cannot submit grudgingly. It must be absent of fear and abuse. And we can do that when we have fully surrendered to the Father because our heart is guarded from any mistreatment or neglect. We do not have to be concerned that our heavenly Father's response to our surrender will be with no appreciation or respect. Total surrender protects our heart so that we can submit without any reservation of fear or intimidation.

Now the words *humility* and *submission*, again, are not popular words in our society today, especially with the NOW movement or with any woman who thinks that she needs to be liberated. If you want to be a liberated woman, it only comes through submission to God. Any other way than that is really a false liberation. Do you happen to know any women who feel they are responsible for their own liberation? I am not sure that they like to use the words *submission* or *humility* as a part of their language.

Another group where these two words are not frequented is with humanists. Many infer that we should submit to ourselves, for we are actually little gods who have the intelligence to exist on our own. (I am paraphrasing my interpretation of their philosophy.) They feel that the greatest love of all is inside of you! So, love yourself, for no one else will love you like you do. But this is all contrary to the Word of God..

The Lord Jesus gives us what we are to do with our life. He says in Matthew 10:39, "Whoever finds his life will lose it, and whoever loses his life for my sake will find it." (NIV) And again in Matthew 16:25 (NIV), He says, "For whoever wants to save his life will lose it, but whoever loses his life for me will find it." In John 12:25 He says, "The man who loves his life will lose it, while the man who hates his life in this world will keep it for eternal life." (NIV)

The key word here is *life*. When you study the meaning

of these verses, you find that the Lord was giving a "double sense" to this word. He was using it first in speaking of the temporal and then the eternal, the natural or carnal and then the spiritual. He is distinguishing the life that we are spiritually born with in our natural birth and the spiritual life that we receive from Him at our "new birth" (John 3:1–8).

The word *find* in Matthew 10:39 means "after searching, to find a thing sought; to discover; to recognize; to come upon by practice and experience" (Thayer's). The word *lose* comes, according to the same source, from the Greek word *apollumi*, which means "to destroy; to put out of the way entirely; to abolish and put an end to; to render useless; to kill."

In Matthew 16:25 the writer uses "saves and loses." The word *save* means "to protect and deliver." And in John 12:25 it says "loves and hates." Here the word *love*, according to Thayer's, is *phileo*, which means "to approve of; befriend; to like; fond of doing." Putting all of these phrases together shows a strong picture of which life is the most important.

So, here is what Jesus is essentially meaning, in paraphrase:

> Whoever, after searching out and discovering by practice and experience and is actually fond of, befriends, and approves of; and tries to protect and deliver from destruction this lower natural life, will actually lose and destroy the higher spiritual life. But, if we will lose and destroy and hate to the point of detesting the lower, carnal, old nature, we will actually find, experience, approve, and protect the higher, spiritual, new nature.
>
> —MATTHEW 16:25

This is the only way that you and I will experience the "abundant life" that Jesus talked about in John 10:10.

I know many times in the ministry that I have quoted that verse back to the Lord and asked him, "Where is that abundant life you are talking about?" And if I was listening to His answer He would most gently say, "You are holding on to the lower life. Let go and submit to the higher life."

In reality, you and I are unable to love ourselves, let alone others, in the way in which God has designed us to love—until we let go of the lower life and take up the higher life.

One of the things that Satan hides from us, especially when it comes to ministry, is the lower life. It is in the lower life that abuse comes, offenses come, rejection and inferiority come. They affect us to the point of discouragement and despair. And sadly, we have a hard time believing that surrendering to the higher life, as Jesus has said, actually works!

What we do is take the lower life with all of its affections, emotions, and faculties and try to protect our heart and mind. We build walls up around the abuse, the hurt, and the rejection, thinking that we are protecting our hearts when we are really losing the higher, abundant life that Jesus has promised us. He is the only one who can protect and heal our heart and mind, and He does it with His higher life. Again, it is only His way! That is why we have to destroy, abolish, and render that lower life useless.

The real kicker is that Jesus tells all of us that even if we try to save that lower life, in the end we are going to lose it anyway. And what will the reward be? Well, while we are tying to keep it, we will be miserable, insecure, unfulfilled, skeptical, critical, suspicious, tired, bitter, and nonproductive, just to mention a few. But the end result could be a separation from our heavenly Father!

We will begin to experience that warped concept of our Father God and the ministry that I spoke about in chapter one. It is only through Jesus and His blood that we can actually lay the low life down to pick up the high life. This is our salvation. It is through submission to the Father, daily, that brings about the abundant life full of joy. I do not know about you, but I want to have joy and be happy in life. You see, obedient children are happy children. Spoiled, disobedient children are miserable children.

EXAMPLES OF HIGHER LIFE VERSUS LOWER LIFE

Now if you have a problem recognizing what the lower life or the old nature is, let me give you some examples through the choices that we can make. Let's say that you have been a pastor's wife for a while. You have sacrificed so much in the ministry. You have to work full time just to help clothe and feed the family. You have been faithful to God with your tithe and offerings, and He has blessed you.

You have been putting back a little money to buy a new dress for yourself because it has been a long time since you have been able to purchase something for yourself. Saturday comes. You have a babysitter for the children and it is your day to "shop 'til you drop." You are so excited! You get to the mall and you have to park in the RV parking, but you don't care. It is your day! You enter the mall and try to decide which store you are going to go in first. Then, all of the sudden, the Lord begins to talk to your heart. He speaks to you and says to bless the lady who has been so snooty and mean to you and your family. He says to you, "Buy her that new dress."

The lower life says, "That was not the Holy Spirit. It had to be the devil because he does not want me to have anything." Or you might have these thoughts. "Not on your life. She can get her own dress. She wouldn't appreciate it, anyway." You might even begin to quote a scripture to yourself:

"It would be like casting my pearls before swine."

The higher life responds like this. While your flesh is murmuring, you grab hold of your thoughts, and you speak to yourself and say, "Jesus said to bless those that curse me and to do good to those whose mistreat me. 'Vengeance is mine,' says the Lord. 'I will repay.'" Then you continue to speak to that lower life that wants to dominate, and you say, "Flesh, you are not in charge here! I am not going to be repaid by the Lord for returning evil for evil. But I am going to do what the Holy Spirit says and return evil with good."

Now, I know that seems to be such a trite, almost ridiculous, illustration. But, it is when we do not deal with the small choices in life that arise in our old nature that will always lead us to failure in the crucial choices and decisions that we must make for the kingdom of God. We seem to have no problem speaking with authority to someone who wants to steal something from us. Why do we not see the plan of the devil when he wants to steal the abundant life from us?

King Solomon said, "Take us the foxes, the little foxes, that spoil the vines: for our vines have tender grapes" (Song of Solomon 2:15). When Solomon reigned, Israel had a tendency to allow her old sins to creep in with small beginnings. This led to her demise because sin will always be progressive if not dealt with.

Let's look at a more dramatic example. Let's say that you are in the pastorate and you are tired, lonely, hurting, and no one seems to care. Even your own family seems to be clueless concerning your pain. You have given until your body cannot go any more. You are working full time just to meet the bills. It seems as if the whole load is on you. For you are taking care of the children, your husband, and the church. There have been small offenses that have come to you over the years that either you have not dealt with or you have suppressed them in your heart.

You have protected them with that lower life. You tried to make them seem as though they never really existed. But in actuality, instead of staying small or disappearing like you thought they had, they had magnified and grown to where you were affected in the major areas of your life.

Bitterness had taken root. Misery had taken up residence in your marriage, in your relationship with your children, in your job, in service to your church, and most important, in your relationship with your Lord. The compassion that once drove you to Him is not vibrant anymore. In fact, it seemed as if it had all but dissipated. You were even having a hard time remembering that "first love" that you once had for Jesus.

The lower life says, "You deserve to be served. You have worked hard and sacrificed with little or no appreciation for it." You say, "Every one in the church is a jerk. No one wants to be a Christian." They mistreat my husband, my children, and me and seem to enjoy doing it."

"I can trust no one. All of the church people are fickle, especially the women. My children are bitter and do not want anything to do with church, and I don't blame them. The only way for me to survive is just play the game and act like I'm fine. Eventually they will leave me alone." Not on your life! The devil will make sure that will never happen.

The higher life says, "Lord, I am hurting so bad. I can't even talk to my husband because he is hurting and trying to cope with the persecution. I do not understand how to process this rejection and persecution that we are experiencing, Lord. Please help us!"

Can I just say something right here about persecution? You and I are not made to cope with persecution. We, who are in

Christ Jesus, are only made to "be happy and to rejoice" in persecution. Look at what Jesus says:

> Blessed are those who are persecuted because of righteousness, for theirs is the kingdom of heaven. Blessed are you when people insult you, persecute you and falsely say all kinds of evil against you because of me. Rejoice and be glad, because great is your reward in heaven, for in the same way they persecuted the prophets who were before you.
>
> —MATTHEW 5:10–12, NIV

Here are the key words: *blessed* means "happy, supremely blessed, and fortunate"; *rejoice* means "to be cheerful and calmly happy"; and lastly, the words *exceedingly glad* mean "to jump up and down for joy" (Strong's).

Now, can you actually say that those responses, such as happy, cheerful, and jumping up and down for joy, are your first reaction when you experience insults, persecution, defaming of your name, and lies being said about you and your family? I can answer that with a big NO WAY!

But that is what Jesus says that you and I have to do when we are persecuted. He is not saying that we jump for joy *because* of the persecution but that we become exceedingly glad *in Him* because that response will reveal the kingdom of heaven to us and to the world that persecutes us.

It is the joy and gladness in Him that guards our hearts from destruction. Remember, "The joy of the Lord is our strength" (Neh. 8:10). We actually have and can experience the kingdom of heaven when we respond in the joy of the Lord to lies and defaming of the world and to false Christians. That seems to be an oxymoron. How can there be false Christians? I guess it is better said that these are Christians in name only with no change of heart. Jesus calls them "tares."

You see, if we do not rejoice and become happy in the Lord when we are in persecution, then we will lose the "salt" in our lives, and our "light" will be hidden. Look at what Jesus continues to say:

> You are the salt of the earth. But if the salt loses its saltiness, how can it be made salty again? It is no longer good for anything, except to be thrown out and trampled by men. You are the light of the world. A city on a hill cannot be hidden. Neither do people light a lamp and put it under a bowl. Instead they put it on its stand, and it gives light to everyone in the house. In the same way, let your light shine before men, that they may see your good deeds and praise your Father in heaven.
> —MATTHEW 5:13–16, NIV

Do you see what happens when we take the lower life concerning persecution? We will lose our joy, which is our strength, and we will be thrown out and trampled by men. And then, our light will be taken from the lampstand and put under a bowl, and no one will see any good in us. And the tragedy of it all is that in such a situation, God receives no glory in our life. And honestly, precious pastor's wife, that is why we exist—that He may receive all glory!

And please get this here: it is not about us; it is all about Him! The real reason for our existence as a Christian on this earth is so that others can see the Lord in us and praise Him! For it was in many of the healings that Jesus performed that the response of the people was "they glorified God." He will be glorified in our heavenly response to persecution.

Now, it is true that He could have saved us and then immediately have taken us to heaven with Him. But He wanted the devil and the world to know this: "Ye are of God, little children, and have overcome them: because greater is he that is in you, than he that is in the world" (1 John 4:4).

You and I must remember that Jesus is our example and that He knows in full spectrum what rejection and persecution really are. Then He will show us how to rejoice and be glad in Him while we are going through trouble. He will guard our hearts. Offense, bitterness, and hatred will not take root in us. But you and I personally must work, alone, with the Holy Spirit in our higher life. For there is no other help outside of Jesus!

SUBMISSION MEANS VULNERABILITY

What happens so often in our life of ministry is that we become vulnerable to other people, and even to ourselves, instead of being completely vulnerable to God. He is the only One to whom we can submit our hearts, and it will be genuinely cared for. And we must hear His response and accept it. He will respond, but we must not be dull in hearing Him. He will always speak to our hearts. The majority of the time it will be through His written Word and prayer.

I remember a significant moment early in our ministry. My husband was thirty-one years old, and I was twenty-seven. We were at a church that had been established for over fifty years, so among some of the leadership there were over fifty years of carnality stored up. The attitude of "We run the church, not the young preacher" was the mind-set.

Well, one morning about 4:00 a.m. J. D. woke me up and at first he could not speak. In a few seconds he said, "I feel like the corner of the house is on my chest. I can't breathe." I called 911 and the ambulance came and took him to the hospital. I had a two-year-old and a seven-year-old that had to be cared for. At that time in our ministry, we were fortunate enough to live near my parents, so my brother came and stayed with the girls while I went to the hospital.

When I got to the hospital, I was scared and in shock at the same time. Finally, a cardiologist that I had never met came out of the emergency coronary care unit with an angry look on his face. He said to me, "Mrs. Simmons, your husband should not be here. He is too young. We are having a hard time settling him down so that his heart can rest. He is too keyed up!"

When that doctor said that to me, he directed it to me as if J. D. and I should have some control over the stress that had brought him to the hospital. The sad thing is that he was right in one sense.

They put him in coronary intensive care and began running tests on him. After about three days in ICU, J. D. was meditating on the Lord, and the Lord spoke to him. He said, "Son, you have been pastoring wrong." Well, wasn't that a revelation! The Lord continued to say to him, "You have given your heart to the people. From now on, you never give your heart to the people. You give your heart to Me and give Me to the people. This is the only way!"

What a revelation! It was because of that revelation that I was able to allow all the hurt and bitterness that was resident in my lower life to be plucked up and cast into the sea. (See Luke 17:1–6.)

The test of that revelation immediately took place while J. D. was still in the hospital. A knock came to the door of the parsonage, and there stood one of the board members. He told me that the board had met and had determined that "we cannot have a sick pastor to lead us." He proceeded to tell me that we needed to find somewhere to go within the next two weeks because they were already beginning the process of obtaining a new pastor.

My heart was so heavy I thought I would collapse, myself! But the Lord was my strength. And even in my pain, the grace of God came over me, and all that I could respond to the man was, "OK, I'll do my best." I can tell you for sure that my response was not given in my flesh, for there was no way that I could have given a graceful and merciful response within myself. It was the grace and mercy of the Lord coming upon me that answered the man. I had determined to live the higher life with Jesus, and He took over in my weakness. It was a miracle that I will never forget!

If you will look in the Scriptures in Luke, you will see that Jesus was talking about *unforgiveness*. You and I have to pluck it up and cast it. It all has to do with choice. And we do that by rendering the lower life useless and taking up the higher life of forgiveness. And to lay our life down means to become vulnerable to the Lord.

And, can I say this to you, precious Shepherd's wife? It is so much easier to do that at the very beginning of the offense before the bitterness has taken root. The hole of the root of a young plant is smaller to fill in than that of a full-grown plant. But in both cases, Jesus is the only one that can fill it up, and He does it with His higher life.

Tell Him that you are hurting. Tell Him that you are empty. Let go of the hurt. Give it to Him and He will fill up all the holes in that precious soul of yours!

Surrender to Him. Submit to forgiveness. Choose to obey the way that He instructs you concerning unforgiveness, bitterness and offense, and you will be preserved. Take the higher life and lay down the lower life. You will never regret it!

Chapter 3

The Shepherd's Wife and Also a Sheep

GROWING UP IN the small town of Morrow, Ohio, I was taught by the Lord about how to be a pastor's wife. I did not know at the time that the Lord was preparing me at the early age of seven to marry a minister.

For so much of our life, we do not realize what God is doing with us until we can look back and see where His hand has led us. That is why we get comfort in saying, "If I could only do that over again, I would do this, or I wouldn't do that."

The psalmist wrote in Psalm 37:23, "The steps of a good man are ordered by the LORD: and he delighteth in his way." The word *steps* is from a Hebrew word that means not only "step or course of life" but also, figuratively speaking, "companionship." The word *good* means "valiant, hero, and prevailing strong warrior." Then there is the word *ordered,* which means "set up, established, and firmly fixed."

If we put the meaning of these words together this is what we have. The course of our life and the companionship (because we are made valiant and prevailing warriors) is set up, established, and firmly fixed by the Lord. And then, what does the Psalmist say? "He delights in his way." That means that we are blessed, pleased, and happy, not regretting the course of our life. In other words when God is directing us, we are happy and blessed.

Although we do not have the capacity of taking our life from its conception and seeing the panoramic view of it to the end, God does. And from His viewpoint, the all-inclusive scenery of our life is spectacular in His eyes. He knows fully what can happen in the life of one of His children when they choose to allow Him to lead.

WHO AM I AND WHERE AM I GOING?

Good question! You may ask this question to yourself many times in the course of your life. In fact, several times you will ask yourself this question and your answer could be a definite "I don't know!"

The important thing to note is that you and I will never be satisfied with the answer, "I don't know." We have to know who we are, what our purpose is, or why we exist and where we are going.

So, here is a great answer: you are created by God, living a Christian life, responding in the position of pastor's wife, and headed for heaven. Simple, isn't it? Why then does our life seem so many times to be so complicated?

Well, a great majority of the time, we make it complicated. To many of us, the answer to this question just doesn't seem to be enough to satisfy our heart's purpose. We think we need more. So we become experts in adding to the load of our life and then return back to the same question, "Who am I and where am I going?"

Here is the simplicity of it all: you are, first, the creation of the Lord. You are the daughter of the Most High God. And before you ever perform even one small duty as a pastor's wife, you are first and foremost a Christian serving Christ. It is because you are first a Christian that the Holy Spirit will place inside of you this insatiable desire to know Him and the power of His resurrection.

That "first love" is what you are experiencing. It was that "first love" that John wrote about to the church at Ephesus while he was on the Isle of Patmos, "in the spirit on the Lord's day." It was the "revelation of Jesus Christ" that the Holy Spirit gave to John. And with that revelation comes the express purpose of our *salvation* and the *joy* that accompanies our salvation. But the joy only remains when we are in the "first love."

According to the Spirit's words, restoration comes with remembrance and repentance. You and I are to remember our conversion, our precious born-again experience with Christ. And then we are to repent for taking our salvation and adding things, circumstances, and situations to it, while leaving Jesus to follow us in our Christian endeavor to win the world. Sometimes you will not even remember how you left Him behind. It just happened.

In Revelation 2:4 the word *left* means "to remit" or "to have let down" our early love. So it is possible for you and me to do all the good things concerning life and ministry and to let down our first love of salvation—our relationship with Jesus Christ.

When we do that, our life becomes complex, and we begin

48

to question, "What is the purpose of all of this? Where am I? What am I doing for the furtherance of the kingdom of God? Where is my life going?" It is at this point that the conviction of your heavenly Father reveals by His Spirit for you and me to remember to repent and do over the works that come out of the experience of first love.

Can you see that our heavenly Father is first and foremost concerned with our relationship with Him? He understands that you, too, are a sheep needing a shepherd. And that will never change. You are still "one of His sheep" and you still need a shepherd.

GRAZING ON GOD'S WORD

Unless we, as the wife of the pastor, realize that we are also a sheep who needs the care and instruction of a shepherd, we will always be wandering around trying to graze, not realizing that our grass for grazing is right under our feet! As you are reading this book, I hope that this one thing will be an encouragement for you, that as you begin serving in the pastorate where the Holy Spirit has placed you and your husband, you will either choose to begin for the first time, or continue your personal study of God's Word and apply His Word to your own heart!

Regretfully, I say that even though I became a Christian when I was a child, I did not start applying God's Word to my heart until I became a young mother. And that was the time in my life that seemed to be the most inopportune time to begin! You see, I did not have a lot of personal time alone. And even the time that my husband and I would spend together seemed to be dwindling because of all of the demands in ministry. But I purposed in my heart to know God.

Because I had left my first love and did not even realize I

had done so, my life became filled with questions that seemed to have no answers. And I began doing ministry out of job performance instead of Spirit-led service.

I loved God, but I did not know Him. And the enemy was giving me one hardship after the other, in hopes that he would completely delude me of the Father's love toward me. But he did not win! God showed me how and what to do to know Him as my Father God, to know Jesus as my Savior, and to know the Holy Spirit as my Teacher, my Guide, and my Comfort.

Just look at the example of how much we love our children! We would not allow them to go through life not knowing our character and our peculiar ways. For we want them to know who we are so that they can experience the love that we have for them. It is our love toward them that reveals our character to them. And that love is not only expressed in giving, but also in discipline, or disciplining.

When they know us, they can then reciprocate that love to us. If they hear us and obey, they will be happy, healthy children, filled with love. And the cycle continues through them, for they will eventually express that love to their children. For the same reason, you and I must know the Lord that we serve.

This is how my Teacher, the Holy Spirit, instructed me. He taught me how to study His Word in order to know Him and love Him. Now, even though I made good grades in high school, I was not a studious person. I did not like to study because I did not like to read. And that was a very dangerous place to be.

The *rhema* Word of God, which brings faith, comes by hearing. Now it may be possible that you and I will not always have someone around to read or speak His Word to us. Through our present technology, we can now experience the

Word of God coming to us through resources that were not available years ago.

There are tapes, videos, seminars, and conferences, just to name a few. All of these can be a resource to which the Lord will bring His Word to us. But our God is not limited to any of these for His Word being spread to His creation. He can use a donkey, if need be, to get His Word across! (See Numbers 22:30.)

All of our present resources are good, but they will never replace the personal study of God's Word that we experience in His presence, alone. The Lord may use these as an early instrument to bring the seed of knowledge concerning Him. But it all comes about in order to get you and me to spend time alone with Him, in order to know Him intimately.

In my case, I needed not only to study the Word of God in order to know Him, but also I had to have the miracle of having a desire to read. God had a real task on His hands! But because I chose to discipline myself to know Him, He placed inside of me not only the knowledge of how to know Him and love Him, but also a love and desire to read and study His Word.

This was how the miracle came about in my life. I started helping my husband with his sermons. Can you believe that? At the particular time in our life, a church had employed me as the music director, which meant that the majority of my work was done in the evening. My husband was doing some evangelism work until the senior pastor (where I was working) hired him to teach the adult class in the sanctuary every Sunday.

This was the "brook Cherith" in my husband's life. All he had to do was study God's Word for at least forty hours a week. He was not responsible for anything but the Sunday morning adult class. What a blessing!

I would put the girls on the bus for school. Then J. D. and

I would go to breakfast at a little diner and study for about three hours until they began serving lunch. He would give me the task of finding certain scriptures and then do a simple exegesis of those scriptures. I would take *Strong's Concordance* and other study aids and begin to help him implement them into his lesson.

Those times, for me, were some of the most precious and intimate times that I have spent with my husband. I was his "helpmeet" in the Word of God. And we became one in the Spirit at that little diner. Revelation came to us like a river gushing over a mountain. The Lord was setting us up for His glory to be revealed in us! What an honor!

Now, you may be a pastor's wife who has to work a full-time job during the daytime hours. Maybe your schedule is different than mine was. But I can promise you this. If you pray and ask the Lord, He will personalize a program for you so that you can begin to "study to show yourself approved" (2 Tim. 2:15). He will do it because He desires time with you more than you desire time with Him. And all He needs is your willingness and decision to be with Him.

Remember, your relationship with Him is personal and intimate. And there is not a form or formula to go by. The Father is full of personalized programs for His children. All you have to do is ask and receive!

THE "LIGHT CAME ON," AND I WAS HOME!

The first revelation I received from the Lord was how much He loved me. He showed this to me in one of my favorite scriptures. (You will probably see this statement several times in this book because I have so many favorite scriptures.) It is found in Isaiah 43:1-4. Verse one says:

But now thus saith the LORD that created thee, O Jacob, and he that formed thee, O Israel, Fear not: for I have redeemed thee, I have called thee by thy name; thou art mine.

Now, I like to do an exegesis of the scriptures, which simply means to dissect the words in their original meaning so that the revelation will become clearer. You may do it differently. But whichever way is designed for you by the Holy Spirit will be the best way of study. This is what He showed me concerning His love for us.

Because we are "Abraham's seed," according to Galatians 3:29, this promise also belongs to you and me. Now, let's personalize this study. This is what the Lord is saying to you.

He created you. He brought you into existence. He cut you out and formed you and selected your birth. Then, He formed you. In other words, He predetermined, preordained, fashioned, and molded you like a potter would mold a piece of clay. Because you are created and formed by God, all creation will look at you and have to say, "God did this!"

After that, He redeemed you. This is a major thing that He predetermined and preordained for you the gift of salvation. He became your Kinsman Redeemer who avenged, ransomed, and delivered you and bought you with the price of the blood of His Son.

And then He called you by name. He proclaimed, commissioned, appointed, chose, and designated you, not in general, but as an individual. Now, you are His! So in reality, you carry His name if you belong to Him.

Now, look in verse two of Isaiah 43. The Lord says, "When thou passest through the waters…" The word *waters* here means "the polluted waters; those things that would make you sick and diseased" (Strong's). The literal translation for *waters* is "urine."

He goes on to say, "I will be with thee" (or literally, "I with thee"; see Strong's). "And through the rivers [or the floods; those things that would cause you to drown; that which would take your very life and breath], they shall not overflow thee."

Look at this: "When thou walkest through the fire." Now, I don't know about you, but first of all, I would never want to walk through fire. If I had the choice, I would run as fast as I could!

But the Lord says that it is not necessary for us to run because, "Thou shalt not be burned." The word *burned* means "scorched" (Thayer's). In other words, you and I will not be scorched or even branded by the enemy who would bring the "fire" in our life for our destruction.

But, here is the best part: "Neither shall the flame kindle upon thee." The word *kindle* here means to consume in order to burn up completely so that there is no recollection of what was set on fire. All that would be left is ashes. That is what the enemy of your life wants to see happen to you—nothing but ashes. He wants you to be unrecognizable to yourself and to the world.

And according to this verse, it is possible that polluted waters, rivers, and fire will come to our lives in order to destroy us. You may be feeling like you are about to be burned up and consumed. You may feel like a piece of "kindlin' wood" (as my father use to call it), which can easily be set on fire and completely consumed. But according to God, because He is with you, you cannot be destroyed. Why? Because He cannot be destroyed!

The revelation of this verse to you is that you cannot be destroyed because He is with you, and those things cannot destroy Him! He is right there with you, and because the water, flood, and fire cannot destroy Him, it will not destroy you! Hallelujah! See how simple and yet so powerful His Word is to us?

In this verse, God says that He is with us in the calamity of life. Water and fire are often used in the Scripture to mean "calamity" water because it overwhelms, and fire because it consumes. And God says that none of these will destroy you because He is there! Well, can you say, "Hallelujah!"

Now, let's continue and look in verse three.

> For I am the LORD thy God, the Holy One of Israel, thy Saviour: I gave Egypt for thy ransom, Ethiopia and Seba for thee.

This verse tells us who God is to us. "He is the Lord, Jehovah, the self-existing God that will make it happen!" (Isa. 43:3, author's paraphrase).

He is your God (*Elohim*–plural Father, Son, Holy Spirit), the Holy One (sacred, hallowed, consecrated, majestic, clean, and pure) (Strong's).

He is "your Savior" which means that He is:

- Your Deliverer
- The One that makes you free
- Your Defense and Help
- The One who brings you victory
- The One who liberates you, preserves, and rescues you!

First, the Lord tells you and me who He is. This is our affirmation because He gives to us with an exclamation concerning everything that is said from this point on. And it is that affirmation which makes it possible to happen.

He then said, "I gave." In other words, because of who He is, He set and will continue to set, or make desolate, anything in order to deliver you and me from Egypt. Egypt represents bondage, which is our old nature or that which brings death.

You see, our Father knows that we were not made to handle or carry in our new born-again spirit-man any bondage, sin, rejection, and unforgiveness. We were not created to carry a wounded spirit, jealousy, or any of the works of the flesh. He created our spirit-man in the new birth to carry freedom, righteousness, joy, peace, acceptance, health, prosperity, truth, and eternal life.

So, here it is, precious pastor's wife. If we carry any of those things, they will eventually reside in our spirit and make us sick, spiritually. We will begin to go through the forms of godliness, but will deny the power of our salvation.

Let's continue. The next phrase is "for your ransom." This means "to cover; pardon; forgive; appease; make atonement; or to be merciful" (Strong's). So our Father did all of this for us. Why? It is simply because we are so loved by Him. Would you not do the same for your children? Of course you would! You would do whatever was necessary to reconcile or to bring harmony into a relationship between you and your children if there was hostility.

That is what the word *reconcile* means in the Greek. It means "to bring harmony into a relationship where hostility was present." And our Father set this in motion for us through His Son, Jesus, before the foundation of the world. Why? Simply because He loves us!

Now, our heavenly Father's thoughts about us were based on these two words—*precious* and *honorable*. Verse four of Isaiah 43 says, "Since thou wast precious [highly esteemed;

highly valued; costly; to be prized] in my sight, thou hast been honorable" (Strong's).

This does not refer so much to our own personal character. But it refers to the fact that we had been honored by Him because we have become the depository of the precious truths of God, Himself. It means that He deposited His grace and mercy upon us, which made us honorable. Our own character or worth did not make us honorable. It was His character and His worth. So you and I are highly favored because of Him and Him alone.

You Are "a Sheep" Experiencing the Love of God

The Lord ends the sentence with four of the most powerful climatic words that we will ever hear, "And I have loved thee." You and I will never be able to negate the validity and power of those words toward us. Whether we accept them and pull them into our heart or not, that will not change or diminish the capacity of the love that our Father has for us. Right now, at this very moment, His love for you has not been depleted one iota. It is still the most powerful force that you and I will ever experience from God. It will never fail us!

Paul told us that nothing could separate us from that love. (See Romans 8:39.) In fact, he said that he was "persuaded," which meant that he was convinced and bound by conviction that was complete that nothing had the power to make a division between him and God and His love. He even gave us a list of things that we would encounter in life, and especially the ministry that had tried to accomplish a separation.

Things like death, life, angels, powers, things in the present, things that would happen in the future, height and depth, or any other creature might all be used to separate us from the love of God. Notice that the first two things that he listed were death and life. It is those two things that I feel are the most important to consider. If separation were to be successful it would happen first in these two areas.

Paul said that death and even life would try to separate us from the love of God. It is not only death in the physical realm that Paul is speaking about here. It is also our spiritual death. And that was defeated through the death, burial, and resurrection of the Lord Jesus. So, physical death can never separate us from God's love. But Paul is also speaking about death coming to us in any form, whether it is the death of a relationship between a friend, family member, or parishioner. God's love will still be intact.

Your ministry, the character of your name, your marriage, or some other relationship may seem to have experienced "death." But God is saying to us in this passage of Romans (paraphrased): "None of that will separate My love from you. It is still as strong as it was before those things came into your life. No matter how dead it looks, My love will not fail you."

Paul then mentions that life will try to separate us from God's love. Now, how in the world can life be used to separate us from God's love?

When the apostle Paul was writing these words, the persecution of the believer was great. Many times believers were offered life if they would only denounce the Lord Jesus. Their own life was offered to them as a separation from the love of God. That was the dramatic side the equation. But let me put it in a lighter, subtler way—that the enemy would come and use the term *life* toward those of us who are the wife of a shepherd.

The enemy would say to us, "You don't really have a life.

You are constantly living for other people. And the majority of those people that you serve do not really care about anything except what benefits them." The devil continues to say, "Again, where is the abundant life that the Lord says that He has given to you? Your husband goes to bed every night, weary of the decisions that he will have to make tomorrow either concerning a disloyal staff member or a carnal Christian that is spreading discord among the flock."

"Look at him," says the devil. "There is so much anguish and tension on his face. He never gets to fully rest. Those people in the church do not care. Look at your children. They are so unhappy. They do not want to be the pastor's children. They want to live a normal life like everybody else."

Oh, the devil is a master at his words of discouragement. He continues by giving you a solution to all your problems. This is what he says: "Just get out of the ministry. It's too hard. It's killing your husband and your children. And they are going to be scarred for ever."

Now, if the devil thinks that is too dramatic for you to accept, he will respond to your mind this way: "OK, you don't have to pull out of the ministry, physically. Just let your mind and heart leave. Leave people alone. All you have to do is dream about a life outside of pastoring. Start living a life in your mind outside of ministry. Start fantasizing about how it would be to be free from the pain of ministry. Nobody will ever know your thoughts. Enjoy in your mind those things that the world can give to you."

I can promise you this, precious pastor's wife, the devil will attempt to reveal a "grass is greener on the other side" mentality to you, full of peace, tranquility, and rest. But the reality is that his way will always bring a separation from the revelation of the power of the love of God. The revelation of God's love is the convincing ingredient, the flawless persuasion that His love will not fail in our life, no matter what life is promised through some other source.

Just as the early Christians were promised life if they would denounce Jesus, we cannot accept a lower life promised to us by the devil, whether it is mental or physical. He is a liar, and Jesus called him "the father of lies" (John 8:44). His promise always brings the sting of death and separation from the power of God's love operating in you and me.

You and I must be persuaded, like the apostle Paul, that the love of God is so powerful that it will not fail us in any area. And we must know that Jesus made it possible for us that nothing would be successful in the attempt to separate us from that love, except our own choices.

Choose His love. Choose to allow His all-powerful love to work in those areas of your life and your family's life. This is what He thinks about you! He is never going to fail you!

Our heavenly Father so ended the fourth verse in Isaiah 43 with this statement: "Therefore will I give men for thee, and people for thy life." He is saying that whatever it takes for My kingdom to come into your life, I will do it! And it is for sure that the love of God will bring to our life every victory and every answer that we need.

So, what does the Lord think about you? Jeremiah 31:3 says, "The LORD hath appeared of old unto me, saying, Yea, I have loved thee with an everlasting love: therefore with loving kindness have I drawn thee." Our Father says that He has allured you and me with His love, kindness, mercy, faithfulness, and grace.

That means that He casts out His lure, like a fishing rod, with the bait being His loving-kindness, mercy, faithfulness, and grace. We grabbed the bait because in it we saw something good. We saw life. And we knew that the taste would satisfy like nothing else. Nothing satisfies us like His love toward us. Let Him lure you in, right now!

You may be the shepherd's wife. But you are still a precious sheep of the Father's pasture.

Chapter 4

Can I Jump Out of the Fold?

I will feed them in a good pasture, and upon the high mountains of Israel shall their fold be: there shall they lie in a good fold, and in a fat pasture shall they feed upon the mountains of Israel.

—EZEKIEL 34:14

FOR THE FIRST time, I thought to myself, where is that "good pasture" and that "good fold" that the Lord is speaking about here? Surely, it must be in heaven. Is it possible to have a "good fold" on this earth?

I was not looking for the perfect church because I knew that neither perfection nor utopia exists in this natural state of life. All I was asking for was a pasture that would allow me to lie down in peace every once in a while. But all

I seemed to be experiencing was trouble, trouble, trouble, and more trouble!

It was as if we would get out of one trouble, and before we could take a deep breath we would be standing at the top of a mountain realizing that it was a volcano! We would feel the shaking and look down and see that the lava was boiling and ready to explode right at us.

I was ready to run and jump out of the fold. I had my Nike Jordan's and my pole vault uniform on, and the pole in my hand. I had already said, "Ready, set!" and I was waiting for the word, "Go!"

I was done! Finished! Fried! I wanted out! I did not want to be the pastor's wife anymore! I had no strength, no patience, and certainly no desire to minister to the sheep who kept wearing me and my husband down.

I had reached the point where it seemed that I was lost in being able to help my husband anymore. My words of encouragement were dull because I was empty. I was trying to survive, myself! How could I help him?

I was tired, frustrated, hurt, worn out, and the scene on the outside of the fold looked like good pasture! It looked like a great place for some good "R & R." And oh, did that rest look appealing!

I would see people who were retired and enjoying day after day of leisure. All I was asking for was a break where I could recoup and regroup. But you see, if you are pastoring, it never leaves you! And if you are married to a person who cares for his sheep and his fold like he cares for his family, every problem you encounter seems to be personal! Every trouble is closely related to your heart because you love the people.

Even if you get away for a few days, you never completely

get away mentally or emotionally. The word *routine* is not even a part of your life. Planning for any get-away always has the stipulation that a crisis may arise in someone's life and your vacation is stopped or put on hold. So when you look forward to your time away, it only goes so far in your mind. Your dream of relaxation has a limited range.

When I make the statement that "you never completely get away," it is only to those pastors who are shepherds, not hirelings. In my husband's case, because he is a shepherd, he constantly battles with releasing the pressure and stress of the pastorate while trying to relax and enjoy the few days away with me or the family. And I notice that it gets harder and harder to do as the coming of the Lord draws near. The reason for that is because evil only has a little time left to work.

So, can I jump out of the fold? Is the grass better outside of the pastorate? Will we be out of the will of the Lord if we jump out now? One thing is for sure. We cannot continue in this state of pressure!

It is a little more drastic for my husband because in February of the year 2000 he had quadruple bypass surgery. His cardiologist and his two surgeons were not so much concerned about his diet because his cholesterol was not that high. But all three doctors were emphatic about one thing. They stated it like this, "Do not get into any stressful situations!" What a joke! I thought they were kidding. But they were very serious! Stress was a killer. And J. D. had to experience as little as possible in his life.

Well, these statements were giving me an even greater running start to jump the high jump. I was ready. But my husband wasn't. And what about God? Where was He in all of this? He had saved J. D. from a having a heart attack. J. D. was so fortunate to have a strong healthy heart, although his problem was arteriosclerosis, which is simply a disease which causes clogged arteries.

The main question was, "What did God want us to do?" I really did not want to ask. I knew that I did not want to be out of His will. But I also did not want to hear the Lord say that I could not jump! While I battled in my flesh, I asked the Lord to give me the answer. And He did!

THE BATTLE TO STAY IN THE FOLD

OK, here was my dilemma. I knew things had to change. The stress level was exorbitant, and there seemed to be no let-up in sight.

I began to fantasize about leaving the pastorate. What would it be like to actually have an 8-to-5 job and come home to family and enjoy your home? So many times I felt like I was only sleeping at my house. The positive side of that was the mattress was more comfortable than the motels that we had frequented. But I felt like I was just visiting my home.

Simple things like cooking dinner became such a hassle. The reason was that, we had to hurry and eat because something was going on at the church, and it involved you-know-who—the pastor's wife. But it was for sure, the dishes would be welcoming me at the entrance of the kitchen when I returned home.

Oh, to jump out of the fold! I began to rationalize and say, "God does not want me to live like this." Now that was right. My rationalization was spurned by my wanting to leave the pastorate instead of changing two important things—my mind-set and my lifestyle in the pastorate.

Now, if you are married to a "workaholic pastor" like I am, at some point in the ministry both of you are going to have to see the light. Too many good works without proper rest will kill you! And what glory does the Lord receive out of that?

I constantly keep these scriptures before my eyes so I do not fall back into the slavery of ministry where the devil has tried and succeeded repeatedly to place me.

The first scripture is Psalms 6:5: "No one remembers you when he is dead. Who praises you from the grave?" (NIV). Then in Psalms 88:10–11: "Do you show your wonders to the dead? Do those who are dead rise up and praise you? Selah. Is your love declared in the grave, your faithfulness in destruction?" (NIV).

The prophet Isaiah also carries the theme of the psalmist in Isaiah:

> For the grave cannot praise you, death cannot sing your praise; those who go down to the pit cannot hope for your faithfulness. The living, the living—they praise you, as I am doing today; fathers tell their children about your faithfulness.
>
> —ISAIAH: 38:18–19, NIV

So, it is our life that brings glory to God. Our praise rises to Him in our living, not in our death.

Now, the problem we face in the ministry is the urgency of the gospel for those who do not know the Lord Jesus as their Savior. We have a mandate from Him to tell the world that Jesus loves the sinner and He came to save them. But it is not left up to only you and your husband to save the world. Your body and mind have to rest; otherwise, you will be in the grave early. And then what glory can the Lord receive for those years lost in a premature death due to exhaustion or a stress-related illness?

When I was young in the ministry, I remember seeing so many pastors' wives sick at the early age of fifty or sixty. They seemed to look much older than they really were. And many times their countenance had no radiance, only the worn look of hard mental and physical labor.

I can tell you that some of them looked like some of the refugees from a third-world country. I am talking about their countenance. They looked drawn and sickly, and my heart hurt for them. Somewhere down the road, the enemy had convinced them that they were to bear it all!

Here it is, precious pastor's wife, this mandate of the gospel is also given to the sheep of your flock. You and your husband are not alone. The sheep are to reproduce sheep.

I understand what it is like when there is no one to help. We have planted one church in our ministry and started three that began with fewer than twenty members. I know what it is like when there is no one to do the job. And I will admit to you, it feels overwhelming.

But this is so important for you and your husband to remember. You must receive instruction from the Lord on what to do and what to let go of! Again, you cannot do everything.

I remember when we were in South Portland, Maine. Our first Sunday we had twenty-two people and that included my husband, our two daughters, and myself. We had five teenagers in that congregation, and they were bored stiff during Sunday school. They had to attend the adult class, and most of the time they either slept or wrote notes to one another.

So, being the energetic pastor's wife that I was, I gathered them in one Sunday school room downstairs (not the one with the dirt floor), and proceeded to teach them at their level. Of course, I was also the music director and the pianist.

Now, there was no one to clean the church, so I cleaned the church with my husband. I worked full time at the State

Executive Offices for our denomination as the bookkeeper.

When we arrived at the church, my husband found out that the church was $5,000 in arrears to unpaid vendors. That was monumental for that little congregation because the majority of adults were on Social Security.

Then there came a few women of the church to inform me that the pastor's wife was always elected (or should I say, drafted) as the women's ministry president. Her job would be to raise money to help pay present and future bills of the church. So I became the women's ministry president.

My husband was also appointed State Youth Director of Maine, Vermont, and New Hampshire. And in our denomination, these three states were put together as one territory. It was composed of only thirty-five churches at that time. That position required him to attend some of the churches in those three states to gather and encourage their young people. When he was gone, guess who was the speaker at our church? That's right—Yours Truly!

Now, some may take issue with that because I am a woman, and I was preaching in the pulpit. And if you are reading this book as a pastor's wife and the teachings of your church prohibits "women preachers," please do not stop reading this book. It is not written to debate doctrinal issues.

The Holy Spirit is penning this book. It is written for you to experience encouragement and relief in Him so that He can work through you to bring about the purpose of your life. He wants all of us, as shepherds' wives, to know that we, as His daughters, are most important to Him. He wants us to know that our life is first place to Him before our ministry!

Now let's go back to the list of my duties. They were getting astronomical. Besides the full-time job and all the duties of the church, I had two precious little girls who had been transported to the cold Northeast. They were being exposed to a culture they had never experienced before, and they needed stability from Mom.

Well, Mom was getting overwhelmed. It had only been three months into this new pastorate and I began crying to the Lord. My prayers were always filled with tears. I would say, "Lord, help me. I am so overwhelmed. I'm teaching Sunday school, directing the music, and working full time; I'm the women's ministry president, cleaning the church, preaching when J. D. is gone, taking care of my two daughters, and living in a rented home that the owner is selling. And to top it off, Lord, I am trying to get used to the extremely cold weather. Oh, Lord, don't you see me in this pitiful condition?"

To my surprise the Lord responded with, "Vikki, that's enough whining and crying!" That may seem a little harsh, but He got my attention. He began speaking this to my spirit. He said, "Did I tell you to pick up all of those responsibilities of the church?" I proceeded to tell the Lord that I saw so many areas of need in the church and there was no one to do them. I knew what to do, so I just picked up the ball and ran with it. In fact, many of the needs of the church, I was actually gifted to do.

I reminded the Lord that the teenagers were bored, that the women expected me to raise money for the church bills to be paid, that the clerk had left the church and there was no one to do the bookkeeping, and on and on and on.

The Holy Spirit brought to my remembrance that I had not prayed and asked Him what things I should do. His response to me was tender, but firm. I had to let go of those things that were weighing my body down. You see, I was doing so much good, but it was killing me, and I was only thirty-two years old!

Here is where my mind-set changed concerning the work that I did in the ministry. I talked with my husband and he agreed: too much good can be damaging to our physical bodies. We cannot do it all. Something has to go!

So I began praying and asking the Lord, "What do you want me to do in this ministry?" And He would always show me, in my spirit, what to do and what not to do. As the years have progressed, and I would have the tendency to fall back into that overwhelming state, He would bring me back to my reference point in Maine, and I would fall back in line with His will.

You see, we have to know what He wants for His sheep. They are not our sheep. They are His sheep. And every fold has certain needs that are greater than others. Every church does not have the same needs. And finding them out and doing what is His will brings about the greatest accomplishment of that particular ministry.

EATING THE GREEN GRASS OF YOUR PASTURE!

OK, so you have decided not to jump out of the fold, at least not today. So how do you enjoy the pastureland that the Lord has sent you to graze in? His word says, "We lie down in green pastures; beside still waters. And there, He restores our soul" (Ps. 23:3, author's paraphrase).

The idea of lying down in green pastures means two things. Number one, green pastures refer to the "tender grass" which will feed the flock, not the grass that is ready for mowing. It is the tender blades. It represents being satisfied and being able to lie down and rest.[1]

Now, in the ministry, it would seem that the pastor and

---

[1] *Barnes' Notes*, Electronic Database. Copyright ©1997 by Biblesoft.

pastor's wife were exempt from this verse that David wrote. But can I tell you that we are the reference point for the Church to see true rest in the Lord Jesus? And the rest comes when we are fully satisfied in the Lord.

Here it is! We must feed our spiritual being first and allow it to be filled with the Word of God so we can lie down and rest in the ministry! We have to eat first and then feed the flock! And for some reason, we constantly reverse this simple instruction.

But, feeding our spirit first is the key to enjoyment in the ministry. It is also the remedy for *burn-out*! Sounds too simple, doesn't it? But again, we must have simplicity in our life in order to recognize the abundant life that our Lord gave to us through His death, burial, and resurrection.

What happens to you and me when we feed ourselves first is that we hear the Lord and His instruction. He will speak to us and tell us what to do and what not to do. He will show you and your husband what it will take to win more sheep to your flock. And He will instruct you on what areas of growth your particular flock needs.

Now, for some of us, this will be a continual battle to feed ourselves first. But I can tell you by experience this is the only reason that I have survived the pressures of ministry. I have to keep Jesus and His Word before my eyes, daily. I have stopped everything to hear what He wants to say to me. That has made my prayer life and my relationship with the Lord more intimate, which has always filtered down to the sheep that are in the fold.

FAITHFUL WHILE IN THE FOLD

When I received the revelation of "feeding myself first," I was involved in so many things. Again, I was working full-time and was a full-time wife and mother. Plus, I had the added responsibilities of the pastorate. So, how was I to do this?

This is the point where you and I with the Lord begin to "work out our own salvation with fear and trembling" (Phil. 2:12). I say, "You and the Lord" because of verse 13. It states "for it is God who works in you to will and to act according to his good purpose" (NIV). Precious pastor's wife, the Lord cannot be left out of the equation. It is you and Him, even when it comes to setting the time that the both of you will meet, alone.

For the Lord and me, it was very early in the morning before my family got up. I am a morning person, and I feel the best in the morning. I love the quiet of the morning. No one needs you. No phone is ringing, and no one is stirring! This is when the Lord and I would come together, alone. I would wake up an hour earlier than I needed to get ready for work and spend the time in the Word and prayer with my Father.

Now, this was not easy because of the late hours that the ministry seemed to dictate. Many nights it would be eleven or twelve o'clock before I would get to bed, so in order to meet with the Lord, I would have to get up at 5:00 a.m. And I can say that many mornings when I would get up after a late night out, the Lord would have to constantly tap me on the shoulder while I was sitting up reading His Word. I was like one of those parishioners who falls asleep during your husband's sermon. But at least they are in church! And at least I was faithful!

That is what the Lord blesses—faithfulness. How do we know this? Well, just one of the many scriptures that tell us that our heavenly Father blesses faithfulness is Proverbs 28:20. It says, "A faithful man will be richly blessed" (NIV). So

I just determined in my heart to be faithful.

I kept getting up whether I felt like it or not. And I know that I received help from Him on those days. I will not know the full extent of that help until I get to heaven. But the bottom line is that He was faithful to me, our relationship began to grow, and I began to "lie down and rest." I began to let the Lord lead me beside still waters. And He restored my soul.

For you, it may be that the evening is when you get your second wind, after everyone has gone to bed and you are still awake and finally alone. Spend it with the Lord. If you have to cut out things in your life, do not cut out the time spent with the Lord. And do not use the works that you do in the ministry as a replacement for the time that you and the Lord spend together, alone. You will get burned-out! For your enemy will make sure of it!

Again, it is just you and the Lord. And the greatest thing that any congregation can see in you is your personal relationship with the Lord. I know that they will see a lot of things about you because you live in that glass house. But the most important thing they will see is that you are in love with the Lord. And they need to see how you spend time with the Lord so that they might have a reference point to a genuine relationship with their heavenly Father.

So, take off those Nike's. Lay down the pole vault. Lie down in the soft grass and drink in the still water of life, the Lord Jesus! You will actually begin to enjoy the fold!

Chapter 5

How to Deal With Carnivorous Sheep

I{F YOU HAVE} been skimming the chapters in the Table of Contents and have skipped over the first four to get to this one with the juicy title, STOP NOW! For it is important for you to read the preceding chapters in order to receive a full understanding of this one.

It may appear that this chapter is written in order to expose those mean, biting, hateful, flesh-eating sheep that are in your congregation. Well, you are right! You may be saying, "You have got to be kidding? Can there actually be what you would label 'carnivorous' sheep in the church?" I can imagine that you are thinking of a few of them right now!

But our focus in this chapter is not going to be on them, personally. The focus and purpose of this chapter is to show what carnivorous sheep do *for us*, not *to us*. We are going to look at the positive aspect of their negative actions toward us.

Now, you may be thinking, "How in the world can the actions of carnivorous sheep be a positive thing in our life?" Well, again, it is all in our perception of what they are doing "for us" and not "to us" that counts.

Let's look at the word *carnivorous*, first. It means "flesh-eating." A simple meaning would be that "someone or something which has the taste and desire for a diet consisting of flesh." Some animals even eat the entire carcass of their victim, including the bones. And when they are finished, there is nothing left that even resembles their prey.

Now, the goal of this chapter is to recognize in the Word of God how we can benefit from those things that come against us to "eat" upon our flesh in order to consume us. But if we will allow them to do just that, to eat up our fleshly, carnal nature, then we will be able to function in the spirit realm for which we are called. We will understand how we are to respond to those destructive things in order to achieve the highest goal in our life. And that is to be called the *daughters of the Most High*.

Now, you may think that being the daughter of the Most High God is not your idea of a great position, unless maybe you are already residing in heaven. But the daughter of a king has all the rights and privileges of the kingdom. And the scriptures say that "the earth is the Lord's and the fullness, thereof" (Ps. 24:1). She also has an audience with the king as her privilege, and she is highly favored by Him. So all of His kingdom will back her up in any need that she may have. To our God, daughters are highly favored in His kingdom.

OUCH! THAT FIRST BITE REALLY HURTS!

OK, what is it about that first bite? It stings so badly. Most of the time, it is so unexpected. In fact, you are in shock when it happens. Sometimes the bite will even leave a mark for a few minutes. And you are so stunned that such loving, innocent, tender sheep could bite you while you are simply petting them.

Yes, you and your husband have been stroking them and telling them how good and wonderful they are. You have been thanking the Lord that He sent them to your fold. They are just what you and the ministry have needed to help lead the sheep to the vision the Lord has given you.

Now, just maybe, you had to steer them in a direction away from the cliff and they did not like it. All you and your husband were trying to do was save them from deep hurt or even destruction. But they wanted to go their own way and do their own thing.

Now, remember this: whatever possessed them to turn and bite you is not the most important factor to consider. Knowing the why of something does not always help to remedy the problem. What is most important is, "How much of your flesh are they eating up?" The best answer that could be given would be that all of our flesh was eaten up!

The eating up of our flesh is a good thing. This is it! Our flesh needs to die daily. Remember chapter two's response to our daily crucifixion. Our flesh is to respond like it is dead. But sometimes our flesh can still feel those razor sharp teeth of the sheep, and flesh wants to respond with a loving but stern slap on the head!

In Psalm 27:2 it says, "When the wicked, even mine enemies and my foes, came upon me to *eat up my flesh*, they stumbled and fell" (emphasis added). Here the psalmist was speaking about those people who want to destroy you and me so that our existence as servants of God will cease. Their purpose is to annihilate us. But the Holy Spirit assures us that they will not succeed. It is not the aspect of annihilation that I want to mirror concerning the eating of our flesh, but the consummation of the works and acts of our flesh to the point where they are no longer visible. All that is left is Jesus!

I understand that it is always the scheme of the devil to annihilate us. And his plan involves coming and attacking the fleshly aspects of our being. But according to the Word of God, he cannot succeed if we follow Christ.

It is the response of the attacks to our fleshly nature that we are going to consider. Our enemy wants us to respond from our flesh, thereby keeping our flesh alive and in control. And he knows just who and what to send to try to get that response.

Now, you can relax with what I am about to say. You and I are never to caudle, pet, or ignore carnality. The apostle Paul did not "pet" carnal Christians, nor did he allow them to continue without correction. He said:

> And I, brethren, could not speak unto you as unto spiritual, but as unto carnal, even as unto babes in Christ. I have fed you with milk, and not with meat: for hitherto ye were not able to bear it, neither yet now are ye able. For ye are yet carnal: for whereas there is among you envying, and strife, and divisions, are ye not carnal, and walk as men?
>
> —1 Corinthians 3:1–3

Now, make sure that you understand that we are not talking about wolves in sheep clothing. We will discuss them in chapter

77

nine. We are talking about Christians who Paul termed as "carnal." And remember, the word *carnal* means "fleshly."

CARNAL CHRISTIANS BITE!

Paul told us that there would be people that he termed as "carnal" Christians in the church. He explained to us that they would still be acting like babies. And what do babies do? Well, they cry in order to have their way. When you say, "No," they ignore you and do what they want. Sometimes they even respond by biting you when they are unhappy.

Now, babies are cute when they are still in the age of infancy. We even overlook a few things that they do that are not so lovable. But when they have lived 40, 50, 60, or even 70 years as a Christian and are still acting like a baby Christian, they are not so cute anymore! In fact, we usually do not want to have anything to do with them. And when you look at their relationships with other people, you find that the majority of them do not have a lot of friends. The only people that can tolerate them at any length are those who are babies themselves.

And why are they so unhappy? Because they want their OWN WAY! Paul said that carnal Christians are still wrapped up in strife, division, and envy. These are all works of the flesh. And Paul went on to say that anyone who continued to operate in these could not "inherit the kingdom of God." The word *inherit* means "to receive the right of portion allotted to" (Thayer's). It means "to be partaker of or to take possession."

Paul said that carnal, fleshly Christians will react in strife, envy, and division. They are not mature because all they want is the "milk of the Word" or that which is easy to chew and digest. They want to hear those things that satisfy their soulish desires so they do not have to change. And please, do not give them anything that requires obedience to the Word of God that will include righteous living. Forgiveness, loving those who hate them, or returning good for evil is out of their equation for a happy life.

Because carnal Christians react in strife, envy, and division, they will head straight for any fleshly residue left in the more mature Christian. That means they will head straight for the pastor and his wife or anyone who is in authority over them. They will take strife and bite so as to allow strife to surface in the leadership where it is supposed to be dead. They will use envy and division to try to arouse envy and division that may be lying dormant in you!

It is because they have chosen to allow the works of the flesh to continue to operate in their life. Those very things bring them a lot of pain. They do not realize that their pain is a result of their unwillingness to kill those fleshly desires inside of them and allow the righteousness of God to blossom. They hurt, and they want others to hurt. It is just like the adage: "Hurting people hurt people." And it is a fact, carnal Christians are hurting people.

So, those carnivorous sheep are going to attack your flesh. But the question is, "Is your flesh dead or alive?" If your flesh is alive when strife comes to eat you up, then the strife that is resident in you will raise its head and counterattack with that same weapon—strife. The tragic thing is that you will never be able to see your enemy other than as a flesh and blood enemy.

Paul said that our warfare is not with flesh and blood (Eph. 6:12) and that the weapons of the warfare are not "carnal" or fleshly (2 Cor. 10:4). But when we have any residue of strife, division, envy, jealousy, rejection, or any other work of the flesh not dead in our life, then we will fight people, and we will use carnal weapons that destroy instead of diffuse and correct.

ARE YOU A "DEAD" CARCASS?

I hope you are. But most importantly, the Lord hopes that you are. When strife, envy, jealousy, hatred, or any other work of the flesh comes knocking at the door of our spirit, all He wants them to find is dead flesh. The only thing that He wants alive in us is the fruit of the spirit. He wants love, joy, peace, long-suffering, goodness, gentleness, faith, meekness, and self-control to be the only things standing when our fleshly nature is being consumed. And believe me when I say that only comes about when our fleshly will and desires are eaten up!

If you are a pastor's wife who has reacted to strife, with strife, you can change right now and begin the healing process in your life. No one can make that choice for you. You make that choice with the Holy Spirit guiding you by His truth. And the truth of it all is that strife will eventually make you sick spiritually and possibly even physically!

Remember what we have already learned about being dead. When you are dead to worldly things, you have no participation in them. Your reaction has no resemblance to them. In fact, you cannot react in strife because you have made the choice to be dead to envy, strife, and jealousy. You are dead to them. Your mouth will not move, nor will your hand rise in response to them, because you are just a dead carcass.

But if you choose to be a living carcass to those worldly strongholds, you are the one who will be hurt in the end. Instead of lashing back upon those who have tried to inflict their pain on you, you will actually be whipping your own self. In actuality, you hurt no one but yourself. And self-inflicted pain is the worst pain you will ever experience. When you are dead to the works of the flesh, then and only then will you be able to model for your sheep the life of Jesus Christ.

DON'T BITE BACK!

My husband has this little saying that he quotes quite often, "If you will give a Christian enough time, they will eventually do what is right!" Now, whether you realize this or not, your heavenly Father uses this phrase in your case and mine on a daily basis. If He did not, we would be doomed to His judgment and wrath when we made the first mistake or sin after we were saved. But it is His mercy and grace that are continually operating on our behalf.

His Word says that His mercies are renewed to us every morning. Lamentations 3:23–24 says, "It is of the Lords' mercies that we are not consumed, because his compassions fail not. They are new every morning: great is thy faithfulness."

The psalmist writes that we are not utterly destroyed for the first sin that we commit because of the Lord's kindness and His tender mercies (compassions) that will not fail. Personally, I believe that it is not so much the sin that we commit that illustrates His tender love and mercy toward us. But I feel that God's reaction to the sin nature in general would be enough to expose to us how much He loves us.

We still have this concept that the Lord is seeing what we do wrong instead of who we are as lost sheep. It is the sin nature in us that He is most concerned about. What we do wrong is the product of the nature that is inside our heart.

So when you and I are not struck down by lightning when we commit a sin, be thankful unto God for His tender mercies, His loving kindness, and faithfulness to us. For it is by those characteristics of our heavenly Father that we are not destroyed! And that means all of us included!

GOD'S WAY WITH "FLESH-EATING" SHEEP

OK, what does the Lord say about carnivorous sheep? His Word says, "His thoughts and ways are higher than ours" (Isa. 55:9). In other words, His ways are more reliable, more powerful, not fickle, and so far above the way that we would respond in a situation.

Paul wrote that the love of God never fails. So our response to strife, envy, and jealousy must be a response motivated by the love of God. If you or your husband have to rebuke or reprove a baby Christian, the rebuke or correction must be motivated by the love of God. Whatever action you take, it must be with the absence of strife, envy, revenge, or hatred. And you can be assured wherever the love of God is operating, those latter things are not present.

Division will not stop with a bad attitude or hurt feelings. But it brings with it heresies. For the Scripture says that where division exists, heresies also exist. (See 1 Corinthians 11:18–19.) *Heresy* is simply having an opinion or belief different than the truth. It is here that dissensions come, and that from differences of opinions or aims or goals.

When we as Christians choose our opinion to be truth, instead of God's Word being truth, heresies will arise and division is the result. And division has a deadly bite! (We will talk about this in chapter 10, *When the Sheep Divide*.)

So God's way is love and mercy. And love and mercy are full of truth and correction. You do not discipline your children to destroy them. You discipline them to correct them, so they will not suffer the consequences of their wrongdoing. And when you correct your children, there is no guarantee they are going to like you for it. In fact they will be most likely be upset at the correction. They may not show you outwardly how they are feeling, but inwardly they are calling you all kinds of names!

Make no mistake. Doing wrong brings pain in many forms. And having to correct will also bring pain. But the pain of correction has the ability to heal, with a result that can come about quickly and correctly.

Look at it like this. If you are a thief and you steal things, eventually you will get caught and experience the pain of jail or prison. If you continue to cause strife and envy in a relationship, you will eventually experience the pain of separation from that relationship. And most of the time, you will blame the other person for your pain when it is, again, self-inflicted.

You and I must remember that God loves those carnivorous sheep the same as He loves you and me. The difference is that He sees the whole scope of the damage that they are inflicting on themselves. He tells us that if we will only operate in His love toward them, then the possibility of understanding is greater concerning the power of God's love working in their life.

If they see the love of Jesus in you and me, they may be more apt not to bite the next time. For His love has the power to reveal what is destroying them on the inside. The power of revelation can cause them to recognize and feel conviction, and then to repent. That means restoration instead of retaliation. And that is what we are called to.

Our heavenly Father has reconciled us to Himself through His Son, Jesus Christ. This is what the Holy Spirit says through the apostle Paul:

> All this is from God, who reconciled us to himself through Christ and gave us the ministry of reconciliation: that God was reconciling the world to himself in Christ, not counting men's sins against them. And he has committed to us the message of reconciliation.
> —2 CORINTHIANS, 5:18–19, NIV

Again, remember what *reconciliation* means: "to bring harmony into a relationship where hostility was once present."

Now it is so much easier for us to see someone else needing harmony with God than us needing harmony! For, after all, we are the shepherd's wife! It is for sure, we are not hostile with the Lord. In fact, we have been harmonious with Him all of our life. Do not ever let this lie take root in you, precious pastor's wife. For we have "all sinned and come short of the glory of God" (Rom. 3:23). The truth is that we are going to be held more accountable for our reactions to those biting sheep because we know better!

The Answer Is: Just "Detooth" Them!

Now, how do you de-tooth sheep? Well, it can only be done with little or no pain if Novocaine is administered. And the Novocaine that we use in the case of carnality is the love of God. For its numbing abilities never fail! Remember these important facts:

- God loves them like He loves you.

- And you are responsible to operate in that love as an example for the sheep.

- We are to rebuke and correct, only in His love, for we will be held accountable for our actions.

- If we are dead to strife, envy, jealousy, and hatred, then they will simply eat up our dead carcass. All that will remain visible to them will be love, joy, peace, longsuffering, gentleness, meekness, and temperance.

- When they see those things in us, their potential to change will be put into motion. But if they see in us what they are exhibiting, they can never see what it means about the love of God never failing. All they will see is a "sounding brass and tinkling cymbal."

That is how you de-tooth a sheep. You do it with the love of God as the instrument for extraction. His love can take the bite out of those precious sheep! He gave His life for them, and He knows the damage they are doing to themselves.

And honestly, can you not see how miserable they are? Most of the time their lives are so messed up. They are either at odds with their family, employers, coworkers, other members of the church, or any other relationship they are involved in. Their whole life is full of hurts of the past.

Now, they may try to disguise it with control, arrogance, manipulation, or even with a passive aggressive demeanor. But either way, they want to strike back, especially to those who are in leadership and have the authority over their spiritual life.

Sometimes there are "biting sheep" who have a great deal of wealth or power and prestige in their life. They somehow use these benefits as leverage, convinced that they have the sole right to bite and bite hard. But remember this: sheep are sheep. And no position, wealth, or power gives any of them the right to snap at anyone. You must correct them, just like you correct all of the other sheep of the flock—in the love of God!

WISDOM TO KNOW WHAT TO DO

I do not know how many times I have used James 1:5 (NIV) in my prayer time with the Lord. The scripture says, "If any of you lacks wisdom, he should ask God, who gives generously to all without finding fault, and it will be given to him." When I would pray this prayer in faith, the Lord would always supply His wisdom to me. And the majority of the time, His wisdom was so supernatural that my intellect was not even a mitigating factor. I could have never thought of such a miraculous way of doing things. But it was always my responsibility to apply that wisdom to my life first and then to any situation that I was facing.

When you and I receive His wisdom and then do what He advises, there still may be a great deal of pain that follows with doing the will of God. But the grace that He supplies to you through His wisdom will bring such peace to your heart through the fixing process.

James went on to say that with wisdom comes peace and mercy. James 3:17 (NIV) says, "But the wisdom that comes from heaven is first of all pure; then peace-loving, considerate, submissive, full of mercy and good fruit, impartial and sincere." Every night before J. D. and I go to bed, I put his pillow in my lap, and he lays his head on the pillow. I sit up in the bed and reach over on my nightstand and get the small bottle of anointing oil, and quietly and tenderly anoint him and pray for him. My prayer is always for wisdom, strength, encouragement, and discernment.

I ask the Lord for sweet sleep and rest so that he will be able to do the tasks that he faces the next day. And I pray that he will know how to react in the Spirit with the situations that will arise in the ministry. I ask the Lord for mercy and grace to follow him and for the strength of the joy of the Lord to encourage him in all of the negative things that come his way.

Now, grant you, many times when I have prayed for him, I was also praying for myself. Because when those hurting sheep bite him, it is as if they were biting me and leaving a deep tooth mark in my heart. I used to tell people that I am not as sweet as my husband is.

I can truthfully say that I have learned how to love with the love of God by my husband's example. He is the greatest example of how to walk in the love of God that I have ever seen in anyone. And I say that without any reservations.

He has suffered a lot of pain many times for having to make a stand for what was right, for having to walk in the love of God. And when he would make those painful decisions, many times he was standing alone. But God was with him and has always vindicated him. I saw how God's love did not fail him.

When the pain of the ministry would seem to be so unbearable, when people would be so cruel and he would return their cruelty with kindness, and when the enemy would try to use delusion to separate J. D. from the love of God, I saw firsthand the power of the love of God consuming strife, envy, hatred, and jealousy.

Not only was there the pain of people being cruel or carnal, but also there was pain that came from seeing the sheep under his care wandering away from the fold. Now they would use several excuses like, "God has spoken to me that it is my time to leave and go to another church." God would always be the One to blame.

Or they would say things like, "I'm just not being fed here" or "My gift is just not being used here in this church. I need to go over across town and use my gift for the Lord." Never were you ever given the real reason for their wanting to leave. And most generally, there was always some anger, bitterness, or rebellion attached to their decision, whether it was visible or hidden.

In chapter ten, *When the Sheep Divide*, you will see how even in separation, the love of God will not fail. In all of our weaknesses and faults, if we choose to walk in His love, it will not fail us!

Now, my husband is a people person. He loves people. And I have never met anyone who wants the best for everyone like he does. But he knows that the best requires discipline, correction, and reproof. And carnivorous sheep do not like to be told what to do or not to do or even be advised in anything.

If you have been a Christian a long time and possibly have been in the ministry for years and still do not understand how to operate in the love of God, just pray and ask Him to help you. He will teach you His love. He is love, for He is the One who gives the description for agape love. He is the expert in giving and showing us how to love with His love. And He is going to do it in your life with hands-on experience. You are definitely going to become a "doer" in that love.

It does not matter if you were loved or not loved as a child. It does not matter if you never had someone as a teacher or even a life example of how to love. Your status in life will never be used against you when it comes to knowing how to give and receive the love of your heavenly Father. He is not partial to any one of His children.

Remember, His love is smeared over our hearts by His Holy Spirit. So His love is already there. We just have to know how to walk in that love in order to give it to someone else. It requires obedience to His Word.

Again, it is the relationship that you and your heavenly Father have through His Son, Jesus Christ, that will bring the help you need. He will not fail you, for you can even love carnivorous sheep!

Chapter 6

Protecting the Shepherd's Children

Lo, children are an heritage of the LORD: and the fruit of the womb is his reward.

—PSALM 127:3

TODAY'S ENGLISH VERSION says, "Children are a gift from the Lord; they are a real blessing."

Are you thinking about your children right now? Or maybe you and your husband were not able to have children, so you think that this chapter will not relate to you. Whether we give birth to children, naturally, or not, God will always place some child in our care when it comes to their spiritual needs. And to be completely honest, their spiritual growth is the most important growth of their life.

Because our instruction in life comes from the Lord and

His Word, we must become sensitive to His instruction in raising our children. Why is it so important? It is important because the Scripture reveals to us that children belong to Him. We are only His caregivers toward them.

And when you are taking care of someone else's children, are you not more watchful and sometimes more protective than with your own children? So the instruction and discipline in raising our precious children to become godly people must come to us from Him. He is the only true source of instruction and discipline.

These four words will help you in any dilemma of parenting: *every family is dysfunctional.* Now that should ease your mind a little. The reason that I make this statement is that dysfunction comes about because of sin and simple human error. And sometimes, you and I will miss the mark, make mistakes, and possibly even sin when it comes to raising our children. For no one is an expert in the field of raising children, so you can relax and fall right in line with all of the rest of us. The only remedy for dysfunction is walking in the instruction of the Lord.

EVERY CHILD IS A "FIRST" CHILD

This chapter was written in its entirety while looking back and recounting the adventurous life of parenting that my husband and I experienced. And what an adventure it was!

It does not matter how old you are when you begin as a parent. It is never easy. There are advantages in having children when you are younger. And there are advantages in having children when you are at a more mature age. For you well know that, along with all of those advantages, also come several disadvantages.

Because I married at the age of eighteen, I began having

my children at the young age of twenty. We were still in college when I had our first daughter. And my husband always made sure that he provided for his family. His work ethic, all of our married life, has been "no matter what it takes to make it you find a job and work to make ends meet."

At that time, he worked two part-time jobs and went to school full time. But when our daughter was three months old, he was offered an associate pastor's job at a nearby church. He accepted the job and was allowed to continue his full-time student status while working at the church. I also worked as a part-time bookkeeper at a Christian bookstore in the town.

Even though I began babysitting when I was around twelve years of age, I still was clueless about how to raise a child. I knew how to take care of their physical needs. But how do you take of them from adolescence to adulthood when you were still a child, yourself?

Every stage of life seemed to be a challenge for me, but not for our oldest daughter, Sherra. She was a happy, healthy baby and really not a "high maintenance" child. But I, on the contrary, was a nervous mother because I was trying to juggle all the responsibilities of my life, and I felt like I was accomplishing nothing well! I am the type of person that cannot focus on several different things at once and do any of them well. It took me a long time to admit that to myself. But when I finally did, I started enjoying my life and motherhood. And really, I began accomplishing more because I let some things go!

We did not live near family, so we had only church members to help us in babysitting when we had to do things in the ministry where a child could not be present. (That is when you really begin to trust the Lord.) But the Lord was faithful to protect my children during those years. He afforded us with many sitters who loved my children as if they were a part of their own family.

It was almost five years later when our second daughter came along. I thought that I had become an expert in raising a daughter for at least the first five years of life, but then our "little peanut" came along. Andrea was also a happy, healthy baby, but with a totally different demeanor and personality.

She did not sleep through the night for the first four years of her life. I thought it a strong possibility that none of us would make it to her fifth birthday! It seemed as if she always wanted me or her father to be involved in entertaining her or just simply being with her. That took time and energy that was not always available, so I needed help from the Lord.

How could my second child seem to be "a first child"? I thought I knew how to raise a daughter, at least until she was five years of age! But to my surprise I was now a novice again. It was like starting over, with absolutely no experience as a parent!

I began working at a full-time job when Andrea was almost a year old. I had to leave the house at 7:00 a.m. and take the girls to the babysitter which was twenty minutes in the opposite direction of my workplace. By the time I would leave work and go pick up the girls from the sitters, it would be as late as 7:00 p.m. before we got home. Then the ministry at the church had to start.

Many evenings were taken with church functions that required me to attend. But I could not do it all. And that decision was not acceptable to everyone. But the Lord was pleased that I said, "No" to some things. And really, His approval is the only one that counts!

For you see, up to the time when Andrea was sixteen

months old, she had had earaches because of ear infections and was on antibiotics at least every six to eight weeks. It was the month of November 1977 that I remember so well. She was sleeping only four to five hours per day, and those hours were not consecutive. Between my husband and me, we were up every night for one month with a crying child.

Can I tell you that she was not the only one crying? I would sit and rock her and cry and pray that the Lord would help us. I felt like the man in the Scripture with the "lunatic" son, when he said to the Lord, "Help us!"

And because He is faithful, He did. He made available to us a specialist who inserted tubes in Andrea's ears in order to drain the fluid. And she began to sleep at night. (Well, at least for a few hours at a time.) Heaven had surely come to the Simmons' household!

Now you may be reading this book and you have a child who has a major illness or a debilitating disease. Or maybe your child is handicapped in some way and you have the added responsibility, physically and emotionally, to care for that child. Allow the Holy Spirit to speak these words to your heart right now: "My Grace is sufficient for you" (2 Cor. 12:9).

What He is saying to you is that His unmerited favor and kindness toward you bring the strength that you need to care for that child and minister to him. The Lord ministers His grace to you, first, which is sufficient for everything else.

That word *sufficient* means "enough to suffice" (Strong's). It also has the meaning "to avail and to ward off." So what the Lord is doing for you, even when you are unaware of it, is He is causing His grace and kindness toward you to be sufficient enough to avail and give you the power to care for that child with His strength.

His grace also wards off any inordinate pressure, grief,

hurt, and pain that would become unbearable for you to exist under. His grace carries you on a daily basis. It is like a flowing river with an endless supply of water. You never have to wonder if His grace will be there for you tomorrow. He promises that it will be and it will be exactly what you need.

You see, precious pastor's wife, the Lord has to take care of you first. It is like the flight attendant giving instruction in case of a drop in cabin pressure on a plane. They will tell you, as the parent or guardian, put the oxygen mask over your mouth first, and then you can place one over the child. Your heavenly Father is going to minister His grace to you first so that through Him and only through Him can you minister grace to your child.

It may mean that you are going to have to lay down your gift in the ministry in order to care for your special child. There may be things that the ministry will dictate to you and your husband that seem to be a requirement for a successful church. And those things will put added pressure on you because you feel responsible for getting them done. But your first responsibility is to your children. The Father has entrusted their care to you and your husband. They come first before ministry. And it is for sure, the guilt of not being able to accomplish those things in the ministry that seem so vital, is not coming from your heavenly Father. It is your enemy, the accuser and the condemner.

If you have other children who may not have the need for as much physical and emotional care as your one special child, your heavenly Father's grace will be supplied to you to minister to those children right alongside that special child. You see, His grace is a supernatural grace. It goes beyond our human ability to care. It brings with it a supernatural ability with strength to care and to instruct. All we have to do is receive it by faith for He promises to supply.

RAISING YOUR CHILDREN IN THE WILDERNESS

I do not know about you, but I have never been much of the "wilderness" type. I do not like "ruffin' it" as it is called. Give me at least a three-star hotel with running water and a pillow top mattress, and you will find a happy camper in me!

I do not like bugs, snakes, or varmints. I do not want to be cold or dirty. Does it sound like I was raised as a city girl? Well, I was. And I only have one sister and one brother who are younger than me, and my brother was never considered a ruff, tuff little boy. So I never really had anyone in my life who was a good example of Grizzly Adams.

Because I have never liked the wilderness, I have no desire to go there. But I can tell you that in the ministry, I have been to the wilderness more times than I have fingers and toes to count. And those times in the wilderness had a much more dangerous terrain than any part of the Grand Canyon. It seemed as though there were always rocks to slip on, snakes in the brush, scorpions with their tails curled, rains that brought treacherous floods, and cliffs with deadly drops. Nighttime was pitch black.

Those wilderness experiences always brought a loneliness that was surrounded with fear of the unknown. And the majority of the times, I could not look down and see my feet, let alone a few steps ahead! So the possibility of stumbling and falling was a sure thing!

But the most frightening aspect of the wilderness, for me, was that my children were going with me. They had no choice because they were too young to care for themselves. They were still under my watchful care, and they had to "go where Mom goes." So into the wilderness went the Simmons family.

Now, you may say, "Why do they have to go?" It is such

a simple answer. They have to see by your example how to weather the frontier of life. And they have to know how to react when life brings to them danger, darkness, pain, hurt, uncertainty, and failure. They will be constantly watching and learning your reaction to those pressures in life. And be assured, those pressures get quite dramatic when the wilderness is in the territory called *ministry*.

I guess I was too naive to understand when I was a young mother that I was actually walking in the wilderness. I did not have a name for it back then. All I remember was trying to dodge those painful comments that people would say to me or my husband. I had to toughen' up so that those who wanted to destroy me could never see that they were getting to me, at least on my countenance!

There was so much unknown territory that I had no choice but to walk through it! And I was expected to walk through gracefully. But I was not always graceful. It seemed as if I was always slipping on sharp words or deeds that were sent by way of the enemy to trip me up. And it was not long before I began to grow tired, frustrated, and sometimes noncaring.

But what I was not aware of, to a great extent, was that my children were there with me. I thought it was all about me, when in fact it was all about them! They were watching how I reacted in the wilderness. I had preached the love of Christ to them. And I had even corrected them when they were not following Christ's example of love. So it was imperative for them that they saw me as a living example, following Jesus, in order to survive the wilderness of life.

Now here is the honest truth. I made so many mistakes and had so many failures while I was there. And my children saw and experienced the majority of them. What was I to do? I had failed. What was happening inside to my children?

This is when the Holy Spirit really began to teach me about failure. It was through failure that I learned about how destructive pride was. For the major destructive factor of failure is when we are too proud to admit that we failed, or when we missed it! To say "I'm sorry" or "Will you forgive me?" or "I did wrong" is the greatest victory that you and I will ever receive in our experience with failure.

Pride will always keep us attached to our failure. But humility will cause us to rise out of that failure and allow our children to see that failure will not destroy them. They will see that they do not have to fear failure.

And here is another fact. Because Satan is the accuser of the brethren he will make sure that failure in the ministry will be a daily obstacle to hurdle. He will magnify your weaknesses to the point that he will try to convince you that failure in the ministry is a sure thing. Because he failed, he wants you to fail. He wants your children to fail. And it is for sure that he does not want the kingdom of God to prosper in your life or the life of your "seed." He knows that if you win in the wilderness, your children will be a greater threat to him than you are.

So what do you do in the wilderness? You pray, fast, and you listen to the Lord. This is what Jesus did. It is so simple. But we make it difficult by adding complicated formulas to our life—formulas that can never be followed, that never have the end result of peace.

If you and I will pray, fast, and listen to the Lord and not the enemy, we will be led by the Spirit of God. And we will come out of the wilderness in the power of the Spirit, as Jesus modeled for us. And our children will see and experience the victory of life evident in our lives! They will not fear the wilderness because they will know, through Jesus, that they will come out stronger than when they went in.

HOW TO WIN YOUR CHILDREN TO CHRIST

Our first and foremost harvest field is our children. They are what make up the most important church that we will ever pastor. For how can we win the masses without first concentrating on the small church that the Lord has sent us to—our children? This, to me, is the greatest harvest! My children have no other choice but to join me and my husband one day in heaven! And whatever I have to do to bring Jesus to them, I am going to give my life for it.

Your children will be your greatest converts. Remember, you have them as infants in a Christ-centered environment. And they will see and experience from you and your husband how to know the love of Christ and how to live a Christian life. You are their living example. And your example must be the love of Christ in your life.

That is probably the most fearful statement that you will read in this book. For it is by example that they will know that we are Christians. And our living example must reveal to them that they will not be able to attain a life of true happiness and joy outside of the love of Christ. For the Scripture says in John 13:35 (NIV), "By this all men will know that you are my disciples, if you love one another."

This is how we are distinguished as Christians. Our children will not see Christ or recognize that we are His followers unless we have love for those who love us and for those who do not love us.

While they are still children, they need to experience Christ and His principals by your life. They must see that living a Christian life is real and that Christ is what He says He is in His Word. And what is most important is that we show them how to become "living sacrifices" (holy and acceptable) by operating in those principles with joy and determination. (See Romans 12:1.)

For it is when we live by the principles of our heavenly Father that His Holy Spirit is able to draw our children to Christ. He is the one who draws them. And He is the one who convicts in order to bring His salvation to them. You and I do not save them. He does. But our responsibility of giving them the gospel begins even before they are born.

If you are a new pastor's wife and you are expecting your first child, begin now by showing the love of Christ to your child. You can begin by having quiet times, maybe in your chair, speaking blessings and prayers over your unborn child. You are anxiously awaiting the birth of that precious gift from God with excitement of caring for a totally dependent human being who needs your undivided attention. So begin now by supplying to your child his most important need, God!

Now, you are going to be so willing and attentive to their physical needs that it is going to be filled with fun and adventure. But you must not forget their spiritual needs even as an infant. Sing over them. Pray over them. Quote the Word of the Lord over them daily. Allow the Lord to be a part of their daily diet.

How important is this? Well, Israel's instruction for their children was very vivid and concise from the Lord. God's Word says:

> These commandments that I give you today are to be upon your hearts. Impress them on your children. Talk about them when you sit at home and when you

> walk along the road, when you lie down and when
> you get up. Tie them as symbols on your hands and
> bind them on your foreheads. Write them on the
> doorframes of your houses and on your gates.
> —DEUTERONOMY 6:6–9, NIV

Because you, as their mother, will be with them in their early stages of life more than their father, it rests upon you to be more of their preacher of the gospel. And they need the gospel when they are infants because the gospel is a gospel of peace. And everyone needs the peace of the Lord no matter what the age.

So give them Jesus even before they are conscious to recognize Him as their Savior. It may seem a little ridiculous and possibly even futile starting with them at such an early age. But they are spirit beings, and they must be fed spiritually as well as physically.

It is the same with you and your husband as adults. You are first a spirit being. And more times than you realize, your heavenly Father is feeding your spirit-man with Himself. Every time you read His Word, pray a simple prayer, sing a song, or give a cup of cold water in His name, your spirit-man is being fed by the Holy Spirit.

How about those times when out of the blue you have this thought come to you (you think from "nowhere'") about the Lord, and you begin to think on Him and His goodness. It is in those moments that you are being fed by the Spirit of God! And the majority of the times you do not realize what is happening in your spirit-man until the trials come or the test of your faith is revealed. Then for some strange reason, you have this surprisingly inordinate strength coming to you from deep within your spirit. And all of the sudden, you rise up and stand victorious without any effort. It is because you have been fed by your heavenly Father and His love. He knows that your physical needs are provided by Him but the needs of your spirit are far more important. He tells us, "What does it profit you if you gain the whole world and lose your soul?" (Matt. 16:26, author's paraphrase).

So begin the treasure house of the spiritual knowledge of God in your children before they are born or while they are still young. You will reap an eternal harvest that is the most valuable to you and the Lord, the harvest of their eternal souls!

If they are already grown and have as yet not accepted the Lord as their Savior, here is your ministry to them:

1. First, get rid of all condemnation that you have about failing them when they were children. Your condemnation does nothing for them. But your conviction and repentance to the Lord will show them a straight, clean path toward righteousness.

2. Pray for them more than preaching to them. At this stage in their life, your verbal instruction concerning the Lord and His love is not as effective as it is when they were children. Concerning their salvation, your words have to be directed more to the Lord than toward them.

3. Repent to them if you know that you "did" something or "did not" do something that affected their coming to Christ. If you had bitterness and unforgiveness while they were young and that is what they saw concerning the Lord and His church, repent and walk in forgiveness. Let them see that walk of forgiveness. But do not get discouraged if you do not see immediate results in their life.

Remember that they have been carrying this anger and hurt for several years. And the Lord will most often use time to heal the wounds of their heart.

4. Rejoice over them, not for any sinful deeds that they might do, but rejoice that they are "the heritage of the Lord." They are your seed, and they belong to God! Bless them when you are with them and when you are not with them. Tell them that you love them. Embrace them. You see, it is almost like reverting back to when they were infants except that your verbal instruction concerning Christ has turned toward a more "visual" instruction. They must see Christ in you!

PROTECTING OUR CHILDREN FROM BECOMING CYNICAL

Here is another scary truth. Your children are watching you to see whether or not they want Jesus in their life. Now, we are getting rather heavy-handed in some of these statements. But please do not allow the devil to bring condemnation to your mind and heart because of them.

For many of you may be looking back over your life and seeing the horrible mistakes that you made in raising your children. You may see the innumerable times that you failed, doing the Christ-like thing in a situation. And because of those failures, your children were hurt along with you. And they may be at the stage in life where they do not want to have anything to do with Christ or His church.

Do not lose heart. There is a remedy. And the beginning of that remedy is confession and forgiveness. In many of the situations where our children have not accepted the Lord as their Savior, it may stem from seeing you and your husband deal wrongly with the hurts that come because of the ministry. And they may have seen you retain bitterness toward those who hurt you.

The first thing that you must do is forgive those who have hurt you. In chapter nine, *Forgiving in the Middle of a Stampede,* there is the scriptural way to forgive. You and I must first forgive so that we can show our children how important it is for them to forgive.

Sometimes you have to sit down with your adult children and tell them where you missed it, in order for them to see that what you did was the wrong thing. When you do that, the joy that comes inside of you with the release of that bitterness is indescribable!

Now, it may take months and possibly years before they can get to the point of not being cynical because of the delusions of ministry that were presented to them because of unforgiveness. But the Lord will be faithful to you and to them. Remember, God is the one who "works all things for our good" (Rom. 8:28). He is the only one who can show them, by your example, that they must forgive in order to be forgiven. When you plant that seed of forgiveness, it will grow and expand to your children. And while you are waiting for that seed to grow, you stay patient and faithful to water that seed with prayer and fasting.

You have to remember that we as human beings are taught to be cynical. It comes to us by way of lies and delusion of our enemy. And it attaches to the part of our old nature where it grows until we make the decision that it is going to be plucked out. And it is plucked out by the Spirit of God, in the faith of God. You cannot do this for your children. They must do it on their own with the help of the Holy Spirit. It is through your prayers and constantly setting an example for them to see that peace will come. It will come in the form of forgiveness, by leaving vengeance to the Lord.

SEPARATING YOUR CHILDREN FROM THE HERD

You have probably heard this statement: "Pastor's children are bad because they only play with member's children." Well, that is not always the case. Sometimes they are the bad example to the member's children.

Whatever the case, there is always a fine, almost invisible line drawn between your children and the children that go to your church. It is always understood that there is a line of separation between the member's children and the P. K. (preacher's kids), whether it is seen or not. And that line will either be one of the most positive or most destructive aspects of your church in regards to your child.

Here is a negative aspect. This line does exactly what it says. It is drawn with the idea of separation and division. And with that separation, a mark comes upon your children. And that mark is stamped with the words, "Preacher's Kid! Beware of hazardous material." For many times they are marked, with no choice in the matter. Be prepared, your children will not deal well with the mark of "preacher's kid," which can set them apart.

Let me begin by saying that they will be OK if there is such a separation. But it is vitally important to know how to instruct and train your child on the approach to and handling of the unwanted separation that exists when raising the child of the shepherd.

You have to understand that the majority of the time your children do not want to be separated or set apart from others. They want to be identified with the other kids. They do not like the rejection, which comes with the title of "preacher's kid." They want to be a part. But they are not always given the opportunity to become a part.

They not only have to overcome possible rejection of their peers, but also possible rejection of the adults in your church. For if Mommy and Daddy do not like the preacher, neither do they like the children of the preacher. And adults have great influence on their own children's reaction of acceptance toward other children.

So what do you do when they are separated from the herd?

1. Do not allow the separation and rejection of your children to become a point of contention in their lives.

If you have not dealt with rejection in your own life, then you are going to have to allow the Lord to help you before you can help them! Again, they are watching you. But in all honesty, their help must come from the wisdom and instruction of the Lord.

Now, while they are in your care, they are going to receive the Lord's instruction from you. So you have to have His wisdom. What does He say about *rejection*? Well, first of all, the Word of God says that Jesus was "despised and rejected of men; that He was a man of sorrows and acquainted with grief." (Isa. 53:3). Allow me to give you a better description of what people thought about Jesus.

He was "despised." That means that He was regarded as despicable and worthless. And He was "rejected." In other words, Jesus was avoided and forsaken by men, women, and their children. For whatever the parent thought, it flowed down to the child. Jesus really was considered a senseless person in men's eyes, not even regarded enough to be considered a human being. That was evident at His crucifixion.

He was "a man of sorrows." He was constantly dealing with the anguish and pain, mentally and emotionally, that comes with rejection. But He was victorious as our example. He was also "acquainted with grief." That means He knew by experience the anxiety and pain of the mental and physical anguish of rejection.

The root meaning for *grief* in the Hebrew is "sick or sickness" (Strong's). So Jesus knew that the pain of rejection would bring a mental and even a physical sickness that had only one remedy—the Spirit of God. For Jesus had to know by the Spirit of God what His heavenly Father thought about Him and that He (the Father) was always with Him.

> 2. Allow your children to see the Spirit of the Lord operating in your life, concerning separation or rejection. In Zechariah 4:6, the last part of the verse says, "…not by might, nor by power, but by my spirit, saith the LORD of hosts." Jesus knew that His victory was not in human strength, whether it is mental or physical. He knew that it would not come from His human strength, ability, or forcible efficiency. But His victory had to come by "the Spirit of the Lord." For the Spirit of God is the executor of the Word of God. And He is the person of the Godhead that causes our victory to materialize.

That is why you and I cannot take our children's rejection or the pain of their rejection. It takes the Spirit of the Living God to heal our children from the sickness that comes with rejection. If we try to deal with rejection any other way than by the Spirit of God, it will only be a Band-Aid remedy.

Isaiah 54:3 says that Jesus "bore our grief and carried our sorrows." That means that He came to us and lifted up those things that come with grief and supported them upon Himself, alone. Then He carried our pain and anguish upon Himself because we are not made to carry pain, rejection, hurt, and separation. That is why we have to give our rejection to Him. We cannot carry it nor can our children. This is one of the great blessings directed toward us from His cross. When we walk with Him, He bears the load.

The positive aspect of separation is quite simple. Your children can know that they were born into a family that has one of the highest callings possible, and that is as the carrier of the Gospel of Jesus Christ. And with that calling comes a separation or a position of being set apart.

Sometimes we forget that it is not only the shepherd's children that are called to separation. President's children are separated. Even governor and state official's children are separated. You are separated if you are what they call "an army brat." I do not like that term because with it comes a massive dose of undaunted rejection.

The problem always comes when children want to run from that separation and try to be something other than what they were called into. Your children are called into the gospel. Maybe none of them will ever be a preacher or a pastor's wife. But they are stilled called into the gospel.

In reality, all believers are called, but with our position comes a greater accountability.

WHAT TO DO WHEN YOUR CHILD DOES NOT WANT TO BE A SHEPHERD'S KID!

In Luke 12:48 it says, "to whom much is given, much is required." And much is given to us as shepherds, because we are not only to care for the sheep, but we are to mirror the Chief Shepherd to the flock. But what happens when your children do not want to be the child of the shepherd?

Well, first of all we should never make them a spectacle. You help them to be an example, instead! And there is a big difference. Our children are never to be the ones who are lifted up to the congregation or their families as a spectacle to produce the highest standard of Christian living. That would be taking the place of Christ. For you and I do not take His place; we only mirror to the world and the flock who Christ is and what His principles of living are.

And guess what? They are going to be as imperfect with that reflection as you are. So relax. They are going to "miss it" just like you do.

It is amazing to me that the Lord knew that we would mirror Him with such imperfections. Yet He knew that by His Spirit He could work through our imperfections and our weakness and cause the world to still be drawn to Him. How miraculous is that? It takes God to accomplish a task like that!

So what do you do with a child who wants to be something other than a preacher's kid?

You have to understand why your children have even entertained the thought of not wanting to be raised in a preacher's home. Somewhere along the way, they have figured that the negatives of pastoring outweigh any or all the positives of pastoring. If there is even one negative that is raised above any positive benefit, they will entertain the desire to throw away all that resembles a pastor's home.

Now, it is an impossibility to keep negatives from coming to your household and to your family. So what do you do? Here is a list of things that will help your children from running away from the pastorate.

1. You and your husband must not speak negatively around your children concerning the congregation and church problems. They are going to learn enough when they attend church. It is going to take the help of the Holy Spirit to diffuse their negative feelings, in what they hear at church. So they do not need to hear you and your husband discussing it.

2. If you need to talk about the negatives, tell them to the Lord. He can handle them. And when your children hear evil murmuring from others, train them how to take all of their feelings of frustration and devastation to the Lord. Show them that they are not to spread any gossip, nor are they to entertain any evil thoughts of discord. But they are to cast all of that upon the Lord and allow Him to heal them and help in any situation. In other words, "practice what you preach."

3. Express to them over and over again the positive attributes of being the child of a minister. Show them by example that true happiness exists when they receive the call of God on their life to carry the gospel. And when they see you experiencing trials and hardships because of the gospel, make sure that they sense the peace of the Lord, especially in your home! Let peace reign, because when they get older, your children will strive to have the peace of God reign in their home.

4. Show them that with the acceptance of the call of God upon their life comes an eternal "weight of glory."

I want to explain this last one in more detail.

Precious shepherd's wife, your children have to know the goal that is at the end of the call to the ministry. They need to experience that the "glory of God" in the ministry will be their reward and that it is a sure thing!

And they need to know from you that their eyes need to be set on that goal. It will be virtually impossible for them to have the desire to see and reach the glory if they do not see you operating in response to that goal in your own sacrifice and service. And they must see you respond more in the joy of reaching the goal than the trauma of the affliction that accompanies ministry.

Paul's response to the glory revolutionized his response toward the suffering that he faced in the spreading of the gospel. I am not talking about the experience on the road to Damascus. I am speaking about the inward spiritual revelation that he received by the Holy Spirit concerning his affliction versus his eternal reward.

In 2 Corinthians 4:17 it says, "For our light affliction, which is but for a moment, worketh for us a far more exceeding and eternal weight of glory." In this verse, the apostle Paul uses a comparison with opposite descriptions. The comparison is between the words *affliction* and *glory*. And he describes them from the most extreme spectrums of comparison. He uses the word *light* to describe affliction, which would be the lowest point of origin and reaches to the highest point with the words "far more exceeding" when describing glory.

The word *light* means "easy, quick, and agile" (Thayer's). Now, if you do not know what some of those afflictions were that Paul experienced, let me give you a short list. Some of them are found in 2 Corinthians 11:23-28 (NIV). Paul says:

110

1. I have worked harder than most Christians,

2. been in prison more frequently,

3. been flogged more severely,

4. and been exposed to death again and again.

5. Five times I received from the Jews the forty lashes minus one.

6. Three times I was beaten with rods;

7. once I was stoned;

8. three times I was shipwrecked.

9. I spent a night and a day in the open sea.

10. I have been constantly on the move.

11. I have been in danger from rivers,

12. in danger from bandits,

13. in danger from my own countrymen,

14. in danger from Gentiles,

15. in danger in the city,

16. in danger in the country,

17. in danger at sea,

18. and in danger from false brothers.

19. I have labored and toiled and have often gone without sleep.

20. I have known hunger and thirst and have often gone without food.

21. I have been cold and naked.

22. Besides everything else, I face daily the pressure of my concern for all the churches.

Now, those are only a few things that he suffered. That does not include the attack from the "messenger from Satan" that came to him. And with all of that, he makes the statement that his affliction was "light." But it was only light when it was compared to the weight of glory of the reward. He had to always keep before his eyes the reward, not the affliction.

And isn't it amazing? The affliction was with him constantly, but he had not as yet experienced the weight of glory, except in his spirit-man. The revelation from the Holy Spirit was greater than what he was physically and emotionally experiencing. And the major reason for that was that with the revelation of the weight of glory came the comparison of affliction as "moment" and glory as "eternal."

The Greek word *moment* here is used nowhere else in the New Testament. It means "at this very instant" or "immediately" (Strong's). And it gives the impression that the afflictions are so fleeting that they give no lasting impression in comparison to the eternal or everlasting glory that is ours.

In order for Paul not to allow his sufferings in the ministry to overtake him and do great damage to the kingdom of God, he had to be aware of the affliction that was constantly with him versus the glory that was his reward, even now. If he majored on his troubles, he would eventually lose sight of the goal and the victories that could be his!

You and I have to see the weight of glory more than the light affliction in order for our children to have a desire to be Christians, let alone live in the home of a minister! For there will be trouble on every side, but they must not see trouble crushing us. We will be perplexed and have no idea what to do or where to go. But our children cannot see that perplexity causing us to despair with no hope. They will experience our persecution, but they must also see that we are not abandoned by God in that persecution, to make it on our own. They will even see us hit hard to the point that we could fall and possibly never get back up. But when that strong blow comes, they must see that we are never going to be destroyed because our eyes are set on Jesus. (See 2 Corinthians 4:8–9.)

And perhaps we have failed in one or more of these trials. Do not lose hope! Our God gives us the remedy, which is the "blood of His Son, Jesus" and we are able to get back up and go on. And what is so marvelous about our heavenly Father is that He takes care of any damage control. For He is the only one who is able to "work all things together for our good" (Rom. 8:28).

And our eternal weight of glory is as "good as done!" For that glory is not something that materializes in the future. It has always been and always will be because it exists in our heavenly Father. It is only future to us because we are still in this human state. But His glory has always and will always be there for us. And that brings an indescribable joy!

Chapter 7

Leading the Sheep in Your Weakness

BEING MARRIED TO the shepherd places us in so many different positions in life where we have never been before. We are a rare breed, to say the least!

Several years ago, I remember a saintly minister's wife preaching at a camp meeting service on the subject, "I'm Just a Gap-filler." She talked about wanting to find her place in the ministry with her husband and how the Lord began to answer her prayers.

She said it was not necessarily helping in those areas of her strength that was common to her life of ministry. But she found herself more often placed in areas where she was not skilled or even qualified to serve. It was those "gaps" that needed to be closed in order for their ministry to connect and be prosperous in the kingdom of God.

Paul wrote to the Corinthian church:

> But he said to me, My grace is sufficient for you, for my power is made perfect in weakness. Therefore I will boast all the more gladly about my weaknesses, so that Christ's power may rest on me.
>
> —2 Corinthians 12:9, niv

The apostle Paul tells us in this verse to the Corinthian church that the Holy Spirit's grace brings power and causes the world to see that power and perfection in our weakness. We sometimes look at the word, *grace* and see it as meaning "sweet" or even "fragile." We might say to ourselves, "Grace doesn't sound strong enough to do the job." But the true reality of the meaning of the grace of God far exceeds our human comprehension of reasoning.

The Greek word for *grace* is *charis*. It means "graciousness; favor; the mercifulness of God by which He exerts His Holy influence upon us to turn us toward Christ and be reconciled to Him." The Lord says to Paul that His grace is "sufficient" or "possessed with unfailing strength that is able to make us content or satisfied"(Thayer's).

The word *perfect* means "complete; nothing needs to be added to it; finished." In other words, His graciousness and His favor toward us have the unfailing strength to:

- Bring us to Christ.
- Save our souls and reconcile us to Himself.
- Make His "dunamis" power manifested as perfect, complete, and finished in our weakness; or, in more simple terms, He gets all the glory!

You know, we say that we want Him to receive the glory.

115

We say that it is not about us, but it is all about Him. And His response to us is that He receives great glory when His grace comes upon us in our weakness. And the reason being, that grace displays to the world His dynamite, miraculous power through us.

In 2 Corinthians 12:10 (NIV), the apostle Paul responded with these words: "That is why, for Christ's sake, I delight in weaknesses, in insults, in hardships, in persecutions, in difficulties. For when I am weak, then I am strong."

WEAKNESS, YES... ABUNDANT JOY AND STRENGTH, ABSOLUTELY!

Paul was happy and took pleasure when he was weak and insulted and placed in hard times. How do we react? Now to the natural mind, Paul's statement would seem to be sadistic. When he was persecuted and found to be in difficult and distressing situations, he would not allow his feelings or his emotions to rise above the revelation of what God's grace meant in his life.

What kind of sane person would actually be happy when he falls into hard times, while pursued by an enemy that hated him? We have to remember that the reason that Paul could "delight" in his weakness is because the power given to him, through the grace of God, would reveal that the power was God and not Paul.

Paul wasn't happy about the trial or the tremendous affliction that seemed to be constantly attached to him. Remember the "messenger from Satan." Paul prayed for the removal of the "thorn in the flesh." This passage has so much controversy. I am not even going to go there. But I am going to give you what the Holy Spirit revealed to my heart, as it relates to the grace of God.

God's response to Paul tells me this: God will respond to us. His grace is sufficient. Paul then said that he would "delight" and "take pleasure" in his weakness so that God's power would be displayed. It was God's grace in Paul's life that brought relief. There was relief in the words that the apostle Paul spoke when he said, "I delight…"

Whether the thorn would be removed or not, Paul had relief! And why did he have relief? Remember the theme of chapter five, *How to Deal With Carnivorous Sheep*. We saw in the Word of God where the grace of God brings peace. And peace brings relief.

You see, God showed up and His power brought Paul victory, which brings *relief* and *release*. That means that our being in control has to go right out the window! And the mistake that we make is allowing torment to come to our mind and heart when things are out of our control. Do we sometimes become the very definition of the words, *control freak*?

THE MASK COVERING YOUR WEAKNESS
WILL COME OFF!

Do you remember the story in the Scripture concerning the sons of Sceva who tried to cast out a devil from a man? The account is in the Book of Acts. It says this:

> Some Jews who went around driving out evil spirits tried to invoke the name of the Lord Jesus over those who were demon-possessed. They would say, "In the name of Jesus, whom Paul preaches, I command you to come out." Seven sons of Sceva, a Jewish chief priest, were doing this. [One day] the evil spirit answered them, "Jesus I know, and I know about Paul, but who are you?" Then the man who had the evil spirit jumped on them

and overpowered them all. He gave them such a beating that they ran out of the house naked and bleeding. When this became known to the Jews and Greeks living in Ephesus, they were all seized with fear and the name of the Lord Jesus was held in high honor.

—ACTS 19:13–17, NIV

The Scripture says in verse 15 that the evil spirit looked at them and said, "Jesus I know, and I know about Paul, but who are you?" Why do you think that the evil spirit said that he knew Jesus and he knew Paul? It was because the same power that was in Christ was revealed through Paul, even in his weakness. The evil spirit recognized the power of Jesus in Paul. But the spirit also recognized that Sceva's boys did not have the power of God coming through them. So what did the devils do? They beat those boys to a pulp, stripped them naked, and made them run out of the house, bleeding.

Now, this is very important to us as a shepherd's wife. If we try to mask our weaknesses, the devil will make sure that they are revealed! And that revelation will come with the same brightness like that of hundreds of theatre lights. Everyone will see the real you, and your weaknesses will be magnified!

So we cannot take traditions or formulas and expect the devil to move out of our way. Neither can we use our Christian language without the presence of faith and expect it to bring victory. The devil will only move when he sees the grace of God upon us, which operates in faith. And it is in our weakness that the greater part of that grace will be displayed.

Not only does our enemy see and recognize the power of God displayed in our weakness, but also do we. And that is very important. Because when God's grace and power come upon us in our weakness and we acknowledge it is Him and not us, pride will not take root in us.

The apostle Paul was so convinced of this powerful grace that he also said in 2 Corinthians 13:4, "For though he was crucified through weakness, yet he liveth by the power of God. For we also are weak in him, but we shall live with him by the power of God [directed] toward you."

How to Be Comfortable in Weakness

Many times the Holy Spirit will place us in situations that magnify our weakness. I know about you, but I am not comfortable in my weaknesses. I have wanted to press them down, act like they do not even exist, and especially try to hide them from others. But that does not work. Eventually, they pop up.

And really, they are like the "pop goes the weasel…you never know when they're going to pop up!" You can sing along while you are turning the crank of your life, thinking that you know when the weasel will pop out. But to your surprise, the pop always seems to not be synchronized with the song. It is a fact that our weaknesses will pop out!

You see, every church member has their own concept of what a "preacher's wife" should be. I remember, early in our ministry, that I personally needed my own philosophy of what a pastor's wife should be. The important thing was it had to be simple and attainable for me. Otherwise, the devil would get a sure foothold in my life.

For me, personally, I have found that living a simple life is the happiest life. To me, simplicity seems to block out a lot of the frustration and confusion that life will try to afford you.

And while I could never become what others expected of me, if I did not live a simple life, I would also not be able to attain my own expectations. Why? Because they would always be too high for me to reach. I would never be strong enough to reach them because my weaknesses would constantly be magnified.

The result would be that while others would not like me, I would eventually not like myself. And when you do not like yourself, most of the time, all of your problems are overwhelming problems which begin to filter down in your marriage, your family, and for sure, your ministry.

For some strange reason, we think that if we can control situations, we will be at rest. That means that if we are not in control, we will not rest. But you can count on this. If control makes up a great deal of your demeanor, you are going to be a miserable, restless, unsatisfied, unhappy woman, and an unfulfilled pastor's wife.

You see, you never really control your weaknesses. They seem to always be out of your control. You may try to hide them or act like they are not there. You may even try to go around them, but they are attached to your life and seem to always tag along.

MY PHILOSPHY AS A PASTOR'S WIFE

In order to become settled and happy in my life with all of my weaknesses, I had to develop a philosophy of life as a shepherd's wife. It had to be personalized for me by the Holy Spirit. So, again, I prayed and ask for wisdom, for I was tired of being miserable. The misery had come because I was trying to fulfill everyone else's expectation of "pastor's wife."

Because the Lord is faithful, He answered my prayer. He spoke to my heart and mind concerning my role as the shepherd's wife. And when the answer came, I relaxed in ministry for the first time.

I recall being so settled, happy, and free in that philosophy that I thought I would share it to our new congregation where we had just been appointed. You know the drill. When you go to a new church for the first time, everyone wants to get to know you as the "new" pastor's wife. Someone once said to me, watch out for those who "wine and dine" you at the beginning because they will be the ones who will organize the "let's get rid of the pastor." Oh, I meant, "going-away party." And can I tell you? They have a stack of going-away cakes in the freezer! This isn't always true, but it does happen.

Well, I thought everyone would be as happy as I was about my philosophy of a shepherd's wife, but to my surprise, some were very offended.

I stood up on the first Sunday to greet the new congregation and said all the right things like, "We are so happy to be here. We are thankful that God has sent us to you to minister with you in His kingdom. We are looking forward to our time together and meeting each one of you and getting to know you."

Then I proceeded to give my philosophy. I said, "I would like to express to you my philosophy of a pastor's wife because there are so many different thoughts of what a pastor's wife should be. My philosophy is very simple. My number one role in this ministry at this church is that I take care of the pastor. He is my number one responsibility. When I take care of him, he can take care of you. And can I say, folks, I do an excellent job!"

I thought that I would say that little light sentence at the end and receive a little laughter. Guess what? To my surprise there was not even a slight grin. The results were nothing but puzzled faces and a few stern looks.

Not everyone liked my philosophy, but that had already been planted in my heart by the Holy Spirit, and He carried me through every sour face and disgruntled attitude. I had to realize that they were only reacting to how they had been either taught by word or by action. I could not let their attitude become my attitude! I asked for the grace of God and He supplied it.

You see, everyone has a different "Momma and Daddy" in the ministry. For instance, if the church you are presently pastoring is more than forty years old, there may have been several pastors. That means there have been many moms and dads giving them the Word with their philosophy and their own personal instruction.

For each new pastor and pastor's wife comes a different personality with possibly a new vision. They will have a different idea of administration and execution of the ministry. Your only help is that the Holy Spirit brings about a bonding of the hearts of the people, especially the leadership, with the vision and philosophy of ministry that you and your husband have. That must happen first.

Because so many of the sheep possibly have a different father and mother in the ministry, through the presentation of so many different philosophies, they have become what I call, "sheep in foster care." Foster care can be good or it can be damaging. It all boils down to how the foster parents express love to the children who have either been orphaned or abandoned by parents.

You and your husband start out as the new "foster shepherds." And, again, your major motivation toward them must be the love of God. For it will never fail you or them. With the love of God, your weakness will not matter to them because they will be focusing more on receiving His love from you than hunting your weakness.

It will be trying. And for some sheep, they will never accept you. But for those who do, they will feel that they finally have a mother and father in the ministry who really care about them and their families.

You are the mother of the house! And the mother of a house loves all her children the same. She wants every child to reach his or her potential. Now, she may have a rebellious one who constantly tries her patience. But she will never stop correcting with love and leading that child toward a happy adulthood. She wants all of her children to be happy, healthy, strong children.

What is amazing is that her children see her weaknesses, but they still follow her leading. Sometimes she is better in leading them in her weakness, because she then can see the same weakness in them. If she has learned how not to allow her weaknesses to stop her growth or to stop her from her purpose in life, then she will lead her children in their weaknesses. From there, they can attain their goals. They will know that their weaknesses may always be with them, but those weaknesses do not have to stop them from reaching their highest potential in life.

As far as the church where I voiced my philosophy publicly they were so glad that I practiced my philosophy. What it did for them was it caused them to see a happy, healthy, contented, and stable shepherd. Because of the care they saw me give to my husband, he was able to minister to them freely. And those who truly in their hearts wanted to grow in the Lord grew to become strong, healthy sheep.

My care for my husband even touched the lives of many of the women of the church, and they began to care for their husbands as the priest of their homes. What they began to experience was a happy marriage with a household of happy children.

Again, not everyone will receive you or your husband. But your accountability to the Lord is that you must love those who are rebellious, just like you love the obedient sheep. Lay the rejection aside and administer His love to them, whether they receive it or not. You must never forget that Jesus loves the Church. He died for it, and that includes you and me.

Chapter 8

From a Wolf Going Over the Fence to a Shepherd Entering the Gate

I tell you the truth, the man who does not enter the sheep pen by the gate, but climbs in by some other way, is a thief and a robber. The man who enters by the gate is the shepherd of his sheep.

—-JOHN 10:1–3, NIV

O NE OF THE most important things to know concerning your ministry is whether you and your husband are called by the Lord to pastor. And if you are "called," do you understand the parameters of that calling? This is important because you both will be tested to such great lengths that often you will question within your own selves "Am I called of God to pastor?"

In the past thirty-four years that my husband and I have been in the ministry, this question has come up more times than either one of us could recount. And it is amazing because the majority of the time our questionable response to the calling would arise when a negative circumstance or situation came slamming us in the face.

Whenever a decision had to be made concerning the ministry or the leading of the sheep, there always seemed to be a challenge given in opposition to that decision. That opposition would arise, to the extent of even challenging the simplicity of how the decision should be handled or carried out. Often times that opposition would be so great that it would cause us to question our very calling!

Have you and your husband had the privilege to experience this in your ministry yet? Well, I could almost say without any reservation that anyone who has been in the ministry for any length of time has had their calling challenged. And surprisingly, it happens early on in the ministry. Time is not courteous to you by waiting until you are more seasoned in the journey of pastoring.

For when you start out in the ministry, whether you have been educated in "Advanced Pastoring 101" or just finished your master's or doctoral degree in pastoral studies, you will most definitely come face to face with the real world of ministry. All of your insecurities will be so visible, not only because of your immaturity, but also because of the vast unknowns that are a part of the pastorate. You can count on it! There will be things that come to you that you never learned from your required reading.

WET BEHIND THE EARS

You know, I never knew where this phrase came from, or its meaning. But it sounds like someone who was so anxious to get out of the shower and dress himself that he did not take the time to wipe himself dry and left the skin wet behind his ears.

While my parents were visiting us in Florida, I asked my father what that old phrase meant. He said that when he was young, he would hear people refer to someone who was "wet behind the ears" as a person who was young and inexperienced. But in that person's eyes, he was the *Master of the Universe.* In some cases, there was an extreme side to the person with this attitude. He might have the tendency to be arrogant and was considered by those around him as an overly anxious and confident "nut." My father loved to use the word *nut.* And then he would laugh.

I believe that the phrase "wet behind the ears" comes with a positive side and a possible destructive side. The positive side of beginning as a novice is that you are more apt to lean wholly upon the Lord and His wisdom and instruction. For the novice Christian, the trust level in God is high and the calling is fresh, without a lot of carnal attitudes to deal with.

The destructive side of being a novice Christian starting out is that when we are young or inexperienced, we somehow grab a hold of a superficial confidence in our own abilities and gifts. This produces in us a certain craziness in attitude—one of "I know it all and can do it all." This disease comes upon us because we have contracted the deadly virus of "I have all the answers." This virus produces horrible side effects, namely, "My way is the only way;" or "No one has been able to do it before, but I can." But the most deadly and insane effect is the "Do it my way or take the highway" syndrome.

Now, you can relax in this fact. Everyone starts wet behind

the ears, for we all have the title "novice" when we embark in the ministry. It is true that some ministers and their wives are more mature when they begin their ministry. But that may be the result of either their age or the challenges in life that have caused them to reach an advanced level of maturity. And through those trials and tests, they have gained wisdom and insight on how to handle certain problems.

Although their maturity level may be higher because of the experiences of life they have faced, it is not because they are more seasoned in the ministry. You see, a person has to be in the ministry before the seasoning process begins. And it is a must that the gate opens and the shepherd walks into the fold, before the actual shepherding begins.

In John 10:7 it says, "I tell you the truth, I am the gate for the sheep" (NIV). So, the Lord Jesus is the gate to the sheepfold. And you and I must come through Him in order to have the stamp of "shepherd" upon us in order to have the true access of the sheep.

It is so simple. If we come any other way than through the Lord Jesus, He says that we are a "thief."

WHAT MAKES "A THIEF, A THIEF"?

Well, let's look again in John 10:1. Jesus says, "I tell you the truth, the man who does not enter the sheep pen by the gate, but climbs in by some other way, is a thief and a robber." Here, the Lord Jesus gives to us the definition of a thief and a robber.

He first makes the distinction with the word *enter*. It is the way that a person enters the sheep pen (the enclosure where the sheep were collected by night to keep them from harm) that either makes them a shepherd or a thief. For the only legal entrance into the fold is through the gate. And again, the gate is the Lord Jesus, according to John 10:7.

Now, if the *gate* is the Lord Jesus, and, through Him is the only legal way for entry, then it is for sure that a thief or robber would find an illegal way of entry. Otherwise, they will be recognized by the Lord and be revealed as the enemy. Because Jesus is the gate, the sheep will be scrutinized by Him, almost like a fault-proof lie detector or sensor.

He knows who the true shepherds are. And because of that, no thief or robber would be able to have passage through Him. They would have to find an illegal way of entry, over the wall or under the fence, but not through the gate!

So, the thief does not go through the Lord Jesus in order to pastor the sheep. He comes about another way, so he will not be detected as a thief. And many times, the sheep do not recognize the thief or robber until it is too late. Many of them are so trusting and in so much need of care that they cannot see the tactics of the destroyer until they are almost consumed.

A thief can act like a shepherd. He can look like a shepherd, smell like a shepherd, and try to disguise his voice like a shepherd just long enough to get close to the sheep in order to destroy them for his own personal gain. And you can be assured that he will eventually ravish the flock. He will steal those innocent lambs along with the healthy sheep because of his persistence and his keen sense to deceive.

So, what makes a thief, "a thief?" It is his response to the gate. And remember. The *gate* is the Lord Jesus and those who do not come through Him are labeled by Him as a thief and a robber.

CAN A SHEPHERD BECOME A THIEF?

Let me answer that question with a condition added to it. The answer is NO if the shepherd goes through the gate. The answer is connected to a supposition. That little word *if* carries with it such a monumental weight in the case of a shepherd and a thief.

Here is the most important factor of shepherding. As a shepherd and shepherd's wife, you must always go through the gate (the Lord Jesus) when shepherding the sheep. I believe that it is not just our salvation that the Savior is trying to get across to us in John 10:1. We must come through Him to have access to not only the Father, but also to the sheep. And I believe that we have to enter through Him every time. Allow me to explain.

It is not that we have to renew our salvation. It is that whenever we have access to the sheep, we must go through Him. And whatever we are carrying in order to minister to His sheep must be approved by Him. That means from the least program in our possession to the extreme attitude or motive of our heart, they all must be checked at the gate!

If you think that it is difficult to get on an airplane since 9/11, how could you and I think that our Savior would be flippant concerning the scrutiny of those who would care for the eternal souls of His precious sheep? Everything that we do for His sheep should be with His approval and His blessing!

It is for sure that you are not going to carry a knife, a gun, or even a pair of scissors to the gate before boarding a plane. Why would we take a bad attitude, unforgiveness, hatred, an "I'm going to get even" or a "just use them" attitude and try to check it through the gate of the Lord Jesus, expecting Him to allow us to pass through with His blessing? It is just not going to happen! We will be held accountable by Him!

Remember the Pharisees? They were really considered by the Lord as "thieves and robbers." Why? Because they would not accept Him as the Son of God, as the Messiah. He was not the gate to them. Their salvation was through the law. In fact, in two different parts in Scripture, the Lord calls the Pharisees "snakes and liars" (Matt. 12:34). You may be saying to yourself, "I'm so glad that I am not married to one of those legalistic, law-giving Pharisees." Well, can I tell you that you would probably not be good enough by the standards that were set by their rules of law?

Just looking over the ministries in America with which I am acquainted, there seem to be many that are few and far between, with the fervor and tenacity like that of the Pharisees. If you only take into consideration their times of fasting and prayer, you and I could not measure up. Their sacrifice for the law was flawless, except for one thing. They never entered the gate. And because of that one crucial factor, all of their perfect and flawless deeds were to no avail. Everything was void and canceled out because they refused to pass through the "gate."

How many things do we present as ministry that we never pass through the gate of the Lord Jesus for inspection? It just looks good and feels good. It possibly has the word "ministry" attached to it, so in our eyes it must have the approval of the Lord. Or are we climbing over the fence with unforgiveness and bitterness? Or do we have a heart that is full of greed and we bring out of that heart a presentation of the gospel that is cloaked by a superficial smile or "the right words" in order to consume things because of our own lusts?

That may sound very hard, but our Lord is very protective of His sheep, just like He is of His shepherds. And He will hold anyone accountable who offends His flock or tries to scatter them. He died for them, and that price was great. Just looking at what He did concerning our enemy, the devil, for the sake of His Church, should make you and I so careful not to harm any of His little lambs.

Precious pastor's wife, it is a most serious calling, the caring for His sheep. And you and I have all the power and resources needed to do it, as long as we take passage *through* the gate and not *over the fence!*

So, can a shepherd become a thief? Yes, if (there is that word again) he continues to try to accomplish ministry without passing through the gate. Even if you have accepted Jesus as your personal Savior, do not allow the delusion to arise in your heart that you can enter the sheepfold and have access to the sheep any other way than always through Him!

The scripture says in John 10:9, "I am the door: by me if any man enter in, he shall be saved, and shall go in and out, and find pasture." The words *go in and out* were often used as an Old Testament expression for "a leader."[1] It also referred to the flocks that were led by still waters and green pastures. Here the shepherd leads the flock to those places where they have access to nourishment and rest. And then they return to the fold, through the gate, safe and secure.

There is such liberty that comes with pastoring, when you understand the job description given by the Chief Shepherd. He says that we must always go through Him, and then we are able to find, through Him, the food and rest that will satisfy every need that we as human beings have.

In times of trouble, we will still have peace. In times of discouragement, we will still be full of His Word, the Bread of Life. When we are rejected, we can be happy because we are

[1] *The Wycliffe Bible Commentary*, Electronic Database. Copyright © 1962 by Moody Press.

never rejected by the Gate. We can always have access to enter in to Him. He will never reject us.

CAN A THIEF BE REHABILITATED?

Yes. But you must remember. Rehabilitation gets harder the longer a thief stays a thief. You have to understand that in the mind of a thief it is easier doing what he does in stealing than working for an employer, being obedient and under authority, and receiving wages. To the thief, honest work is too taxing and it does not pay enough. The thief always feels as though there is a better, easier way to accomplish what he needs. To the thief, honest work is not the answer. A thief has no authority except himself—until he gets caught! And the severity of his punishment for his crimes is bondage, not freedom. He can no longer do what he wants to do.

A thief is not interested in the persons from whom he is stealing. He is not concerned with their welfare or their pain. And if a thief becomes a robber, then he not only steals but he also ravishes and destroys whatever he leaves behind. He has no conscience, for it is all about him!

Now, in order for a thief to be rehabilitated, two important things must happen. Number one, the thief has to come to himself and be convicted of what he has done. He has to see that he has been a thief, *a convict,* and that what he has been doing is wrong. Unless he sees his sin, then he can never do step number two. And step two is he must repent and live lawfully. How simple can it be?

In the case of a shepherd, he must not spurn the conviction of the Holy Spirit concerning his thievery. Now I am not speaking of a situation where a pastor has either stolen money or misappropriated funds. That is the horrible extreme of thievery. It is the small promptings of conviction that the

Holy Spirit uses concerning ministering to the flock that I want to address.

An example of where a pastor (shepherd) would begin to "climb over the fence" instead of "go through the gate" would be in replacing "worship or ministry" with "performance." You may be asking, "What do you mean by 'performance or performing?'" Well, let's take the position of an actor or actress. They perform to entertain and to receive accolades for themselves. The applause of men is their fulfilling reward.

If a shepherd ever begins to perform his or her ministry, you can be assured that that performance did not pass through the gate. Our Lord Jesus never performed for the sheep, and he will never allow us to. For you see, performance has little or no changing effect on the audience. But it only puffs up the performer. The performer is the recipient, and the audience is being used for the gratification of the performer.

Do not get me wrong! The principles of our Lord will work, even in performance. But eventually, the performer will be seen without the principles operating in his own life. And the audience will simply see him as an actor. Then those principles have the potential of looking superficial to those who are observing the performance. The life-giving teachings of our Lord will then seem to be unreal and unattainable.

Jesus gave His life for the sheep. His life was given for all of us and that never came by way of entertainment. For what He did for us consisted of suffering, rejection, and pain. But His sole gratification was that we had the opportunity to be reconciled to the Heavenly Father through Him, to live with Him for eternity. We are His reward.

Now, when you and I begin any ministry to the flock where

the Lord has planted us, it must be without performance. And as long as what we do is passed through the gate of the Lord Jesus, we will always stay as His under-shepherd. And we will see the same results that He sees—many souls!

So, leave performance behind, for it will cause you to believe that there is a certain formula to go by in shepherding. It really is futile for us to just pick up a book on church growth and expect those same formulas that one pastor used to always work where we are planted. The same principles of God will be exhibited, but they will most probably be with a different format.

People are different in different parts of the country in respect to certain needs of their life. And some things that worked for the pastor in the metropolitan area of Los Angeles will not work in the rural area of Bybee, Kentucky. The Holy Spirit has a plan for His flock. Anything outside of His plan will border on thievery.

If we have been guilty of performance or simply "doing it our way," all we have to do is allow the conviction of the Holy Spirit to bring us to repentance—or that place of entering the pastorate through the gate, His way.

CHANGING FROM A THIEF TO A SHEPHERD

There must be a change. That is the purpose of rehabilitation. In John, chapter three, we have the story of a man who was in the position of *thief* but changed into a *shepherd*:

> Now there was a man of the Pharisees named Nicodemus, a member of the Jewish ruling council. He came to Jesus at night and said, "Rabbi, we know you are a teacher who has come from God. For no one could perform the miraculous signs you are doing if God were not with him. In reply Jesus declared, "I tell

you the truth, no one can see the kingdom of God
unless he is born again.

—JOHN 3:1–3, NIV

The main point of these scriptures is that it only took
one sentence given by Jesus to reveal to Nicodemus where
he stood his entire life as a religious man. Isn't it interesting that Nicodemus addressed Jesus in the position of rabbi,
and the response from Jesus was ignored? It was almost like
Nicodemus had said nothing to the Lord. For the response
basically from Jesus was, "Let's look at where you are,
Nicodemus" (author's paraphrase).

You are never going to have to wonder where you stand, as
far as the Lord is concerned. The Holy Spirit is bound by His
Word to convict and prompt us toward His ways and principles of heaven. He will never allow us to just take shots in the
dark concerning the care of the souls of His precious sheep.
He will reveal our sin and any distraction that would lead us to
sin, for not only His sake, but also for the sake of His flock.

He is not going to allow you and me to go on our own
without revealing to us our error in judgment and the consequences of that path. He will make sure that the small errors
will be revealed quickly so that they do not lead into larger,
more destructive errors. He loves us and it is for sure that
through His salvation "He is able to present us faultless and
keep us from falling" (Jude 24).

Note how Jesus did not respond to Nicodemus about what
he did right or what he did wrong in the ministry of being
a Pharisee. He did not comment on whether he had been a
good person or if had done good deeds. Jesus went straight
to the condition of Nicodemus's soul. He basically said (paraphrased), "Nicodemus, you are going to have to go through

the gate." He was saying that everything outside of the gate is wrong. All of the religious, lawful things that Nicodemus had done up to that point really availed to nothing, unless he went through the gate. The ministry that Nicodemus had performed, even to the letter of the law, was thievery, unless he passed through the gate.

The gate, the gate, the gate—that is the only passage way to the sheep that is acceptable by God. And it is, for sure, that our enemy, and even our flesh, will try to divert our way from the gate to over the fence and down the wall.

Being a shepherd's wife puts so many demands on our life. Just the appearance of our position reflects a superficial, flawless, wonder-woman-type syndrome in the eyes of the congregation. They want us perfect, gifted, sweet, kind, loving, beautiful, stylish, talented, and wise. We are to be the perfect mother, the perfect wife, and especially the perfect pastor's wife. And the real irony of all of this is if we are "too good" then they hate us for being "too perfect." It is a no-win situation.

It is possible that what the Lord has given to us for His sheep, some of them will feel it is not adequate, so your "approval ratings" plummet in their eyes. But His approval is always enough. Anything more will just spoil the sheep and cause them to become over-fed and lazy. Really, when we feed our animals too much because they want more, it could eventually cause an early death.

Precious pastor's wife, all you have to give the sheep is what your Savior has approved for them. He does not expect you to do more nor does He want you to do more. If you and I do more than we are expected to do, the load will get too heavy for us. And what will happen is that we will revert to climbing over the fence with the easier things of ministry. We will begin to perform the things of ministry, instead of giving Jesus to the people. It is a horrible trap to be caught us in, but you can get out!

You are going to have to know what the Holy Spirit wants for you to do specifically in spreading His Gospel. You are going to have to be honest with your husband when you are overloaded and doing too much. Even when you see him overloaded, and you want to take some of the load off of him, you are going to have to go to the Lord and ask Him if that particular task is what He wants you to do.

It is a tuff row to hoe when both of you are overloaded. Neither one of you can help the other. And that opens the door to your enemy to bring bitterness, strive, division, and self-pity into your heart. Then you begin to believe the lie that "nobody cares, everyone wants to use you, nobody wants to help, or everyone is against you."

Haven't you ever noticed how the devil magnifies the idea in your mind that if one or two people are disgruntled with what you do that the whole congregation feels the same way? He has to magnify it in your mind; otherwise, you will see the truth and realize how really small and insignificant the situation is.

The devil uses our disobedience of not going through the gate but climbing over the fence to add to our cynical carnal nature. We start looking at every situation or every person as having an agenda or an unkind motive toward us and our ministry. We think we have to placate every negative attitude, just so the pot won't be stirred and boiled over.

All of this comes from either bypassing the Lord Jesus or believing that what He instructs us to do is not enough or satisfactory to get the job done. Do you see how easy it is to get on the wrong track?

When a thief becomes a thief, he does not start out by making his first theft the bank heist of the century. No, he begins by picking up a candy bar at a local drug store and leaving without paying for it. Then it can accelerate to stealing clothes or jewelry, or even robbing a home, or going to the extreme and trying to rob Fort Knox. So, it starts with little things or little jobs to make life easier and more fulfilling.

Can I tell you that we cannot add or take away anything that our Savior has planned or purposed for us to do in service to His body? He does not want us to be abused or used up in the ministry by the delusion that it takes more or less than what He has instructed us to do. If we circumvent Him, we put our foot on the first slat of the fence. And immediately, the Holy Spirit will reveal to us that we are about to climb the fence and get into real hot water.

Listen to His conviction and instruction. The only easy way in ministry is to pass through the gate. The fence or the wall will bring you a great fall, one from which you may not easily recover.

Chapter 9

Forgiving in the Middle of a Stampede

Take heed to yourselves: If thy brother trespass against thee, rebuke him; and if he repent, forgive him.
—LUKE 17:3

ORGIVE. HOW DO we start? It sounds like a simple little word. *Forgive!* It has only seven letters. I know that you have probably heard hundreds of sermons on the subject of forgiveness. Your husband has probably preached a few in his years as a shepherd. And we know that hearing a sermon about forgiveness and actually forgiving someone brings us into the reality of the full equation of being a doer of the word and not a hearer only. (See James 1:23.)

IS FORGIVENESS REALLY REQUIRED?

The primary thing for us to remember is that forgiveness is an active demonstration of the will and requires our continual obedience. That seems to be a very strong statement, but we are living in an age that the black and white of life fades into that acceptable gray or murky, which is the comfortable arena of living that we seem to enjoy best.

In Leviticus 19:18, God gave the spelled-out version concerning *forgiveness*. He says it in such a simplistic way for us so that there will be no misunderstanding: "Thou shalt not avenge, nor bear any grudge against the children of thy people, but thou shalt love thy neighbor as thyself: I am the LORD." I know that the word *forgive* is not in this particular verse, but if we hold a grudge, we also hold unforgiveness.

If we really look at this scripture and see what the Lord is saying to His people, we will see a simple yet firm statement of fact concerning forgiveness. The words *not avenge* mean "to *not* take revenge toward anyone or to punish anyone" (Strong's). A stronger meaning is to not bring vengeance on anyone.

Then you have the words "bear any grudge," which mean that we cannot keep guard, reserve, or simply hold on to wrath or anger toward anyone.[1] That means if someone has hurt you or done some type of evil toward you, you cannot return evil to him or her, neither can you "*let the sun go down on your wrath*" (Eph. 4:26).

Paul wrote to the church at Ephesus and told them they could be angry, but they could not sin in that anger. One reason is because sin was more apt to come in when we let a day end without taking care of anger.

[1] Author's paraphrase of word definition from *Brown, Driver, and Briggs Hebrew Lexicon*, Woodside Bible Fellowship, Ontario, Canada. Copyright © 1993.

The Lord then furthers the command to us in Leviticus 19:18 by saying that we must love them like we love ourselves. Wow! He really makes it plain, doesn't He?

You know, there may be some times in our life where we are inordinately unforgiving to ourselves. We may have done some unwise or even stupid things that would cause us to hold unforgiveness in our heart toward ourselves. But that holds true in fewer times than those in which we have been offended and hurt by someone else.

Whether we think that we have a justifiable reason or not, we cannot hold a grudge against them. We seem to be much more apt to quickly forgive ourselves than someone else who has deliberately hurt us. After all, we are "our own best friend." We are a "pretty good-ole Joe, or Josephine in our case!" And it is for sure, we do not intentionally hurt ourselves.

But the most amazing statement in this scripture comes at the finish line: "I am the LORD." This is the eighth time in this chapter that the Holy Spirit inspired the writer to write, "I am the LORD." Literally He said, "I, the LORD." Why do you think He made a point to say that salutation so many times, and yet the chapter had only begun? I think that He has to constantly make us aware, just like He did to Israel, that what was being commanded came from the highest authority that we would ever submit to. He is Lord! And because of His position, it demands us to be obedient to nothing more or less than His complete instruction.

It is like placing the stamp of the king on a decree after it was written by Him. The king's signature was the stamp of his ring. It was the highest authority in the land. God's signature to us is His Word, stamped in the blood of His Son, Jesus Christ. And even though our Lord had not come to this earth when this command was given, He was still the

Word made flesh and the Lamb slain from before the foundation of the world.

As far as God the Father was concerned, Jesus had already been born. He had already lived His sinless life, died His vicarious death, and had been raised from the dead for our victory. His life was already made applicable to Israel as well as to us. That makes Him our highest authority.

And because of this, when we look at the command to forgive, we cannot simply obey by our outward expression. We cannot act like we have forgiven when our heart is still black with envy, strife, and unforgiveness.

There is no foundational cover-up or concealer strong enough to shade the darkness of unforgiveness from the Holy Spirit. He will reveal and convict us to get rid of it. He speaks to us over and over again in His Word and tells us that forgiveness must come as an act of obedience of the heart. It is not outward. It is inward. And that inward action will always manifest outwardly!

Jesus said the same thing about adultery and murder. He said that lusting in the heart for someone other than your spouse is the same as committing adultery, outwardly. (See Matthew 5:27–28.) In other words, mental adultery is the same as physical adultery.

He said the same thing about murder. If we have hatred in our heart, Jesus says it is the same as if we have committed murder. I knew that this chapter was going to be vivid and uncompromising, but I am telling you by experience: unforgiveness will separate you from the Father. It is a serious thing, a sin that must be reckoned with. We have to give it up!

CLOAKING UNFORGIVENESS

Now, we are good at cloaking our hatred and unforgiveness. In fact, if an Academy Award were given to the best actor and actress for their role in the saga called "Superficial Forgiveness," the trophy industry could not keep up with the need of production. Our cloaking mechanism is better than the cloaking of the Star Ship Enterprise! The sadness of this statement is that the world would not be getting the majority of the trophies. The Church would!

For some reason, we think God is oblivious to our unforgiving spirit, just as long as we cloak it with a smile or even a nice gesture. We have the misconception that as long as we are civil to them and we do not shoot them with a 357 magnum that we can allow the unforgiveness to stay in our spirit. Please, get rid of that lie. It is from the chamber of hell, itself!

Now, we can say that we just simply dislike the person and even outwardly say that we have forgiven them. But the real test of forgiveness comes when that person offends us again. Jesus said that it could happen that very same day. The same offense toward us could come 7 times or as much as 490 times in one day, and we are to forgive them when they repent. That sounds almost like science fiction. There is no way of doing this without the grace and mercy of God, our Father. But it can be done with His mercy and grace!

Do you remember the story that Jesus told Peter when Peter asked Him the question, "How many times can my brother sin against me and I have to forgive him?" In Matthew 18:21–35, Jesus did not just answer Peter's question. He began to tell him a parable, which exposed just how great our sin of offense is toward the Lord in comparison to the offense that someone would bring toward us.

144

Our sin toward the Father is so much greater. And because of Jesus and His precious blood, we are forgiven of that greater part when we repent. That is why the Lord expects us to forgive those that hurt us. Because no matter how bad the offense is toward us, no matter how many times it comes, it will never compare to our own sin that the Father has forgiven us through Jesus Christ.

I never realized, until much later in my life, how true this really is. Because I was saved as a child and raised in church, I never did most of the things that a "hard core" sinner may do. I didn't smoke, cuss, drink, chew, or run around with girls who do! I was a good, obedient child who did not even talk back to her parents. I might sneak and do things behind their back, but nothing of any consequence. I was the model child in my own eyes. So, what big thing did God really have to forgive me for? I was basically good like the rich young ruler.

This is why I had such a hard time in our early ministry, trying to forgive those who hurt me or my husband and my children. Their sin against me seemed to far outweigh what I did to the heavenly Father. For this reason alone, you and I need the same revelation that Paul had—referring to himself as the chief of sinners! When we do not have that revelation about ourselves, we immediately set ourselves as judge!

You have to be aware of where you are because the majority of the time people who bring offenses to us will be so subtle with their poison-filled darts. And most of the time they are unrecognizable to others. This makes it dangerous for us to confront because they will immediately become the martyr, and you will be viewed as the villain.

Here I was, in such a dilemma. I could not rebuke because the offense was so underhanded and sly, and the innocent people standing around could not see what was being done. Why? It was because of the subtlety of the devil's device. You see, those type of people who bring offense to us have their doctoral degree in presentation. They speak to others slowly and even compassionately at times, not loading on too much at once.

It is the building of offenses that the little lambs are unaware of. And before they realize what has happened, you have been degraded and demoted in their eyes as the bully or the nonspiritual preacher and preacher's wife.

FORGIVENESS MAY HAVE A BITTER TASTE

I want to stop right here and let this slightly bitter medicine called "forgiveness" settle in your spirit. You may be hurting so badly that you are at the point, on a daily basis, of dreaming the dream of the ecstasy and bliss of quitting the ministry. In all probability, you have been wounded and left for dead more times than you can count. And the offense has come from those you have loved and cared for so diligently!

Again, this medicine may be a little strong and bitter. But, my precious shepherd's wife, it is the only remedy for the pain and hurt of offense. There is no other way out except the way of the forgiving heart.

I know that you realize when you are sick in the natural; the doctor may have explained to you the only procedure that will remedy your illness. And sometimes, it may be a very painful and lengthy procedure. It may be surgery. It may be chemotherapy. It may be a medication that you have to take that has terrible side effects. It may be therapy that causes such pain with every movement. But you must take it in order to live. The bottom line is making the choice to live, no matter what!

What will help you to know about God's prescription concerning forgiveness is that the major ingredient in His medicine is His Grace. He is our help, our only help. He said that He is a "very present help in trouble" (Ps 46:1).

If you and I will become vulnerable to Him and allow His Holy Spirit to come alongside us and be the help and comfort, we will be able to forgive the most horrendous offense, by the "all sufficient" grace of God. The only side effect we experience is a clean heart and a renewed spirit. When we make the choice to forgive, He becomes our help and the healer of our wounds.

And remember this, precious pastor's wife, when we are obedient and forgive, it is God's responsibility to carry the pain of the offense. His Word says that Jesus "carried our sorrows" and He "bore our grief" (Isa. 53:4). We are not made to carry them. So what we do is obey and forgive and then "cast the care" of the hurt on Him. Peter said in 1 Peter 5:7, "Casting all your care upon him; for he careth for you."

It is interesting to know that the word "casting" comes from the Greek word that means "distraction" or "to be drawn into different directions." The enemy uses offense as a distraction to draw us into the different direction called "unforgiveness." He does not want our heart to even walk toward the path of forgiveness.

The words *careth for* mean "will take care." So the Lord promises us that He will take care of us by dealing with our pain and abuse of the offense. We can trust the Lord with the pain in our heart because He is the only one who can heal our broken heart. We cannot heal it, no matter how hard we try or how good our resources may be. It will still only be flesh taking care of flesh.

When there arises the stirring in our spirit, the unsettledness, the pain of the remembrance of the offense, the precious Holy Spirit reveals again to us the unforgiveness and convicts us to forgive. Conviction is one of our greatest gifts that we receive from Him. He will never bring condemnation. He brings conviction—the conviction to forgive.

We might get by for a while with the old cliché, "Out of sight, out of mind." But that does not work with the Holy Spirit. He makes sure that only forgiveness becomes our remedy for offense.

THREE HARD WORDS: I FORGIVE YOU!

Now, why do you think that is such a hard thing for us to do? That is, to forgive someone who has hurt us? Could it be that we were never taught as a child about how to forgive an offense? Maybe this simple illustration will help us understand.

How many times have you had to take one of your children who has hurt his/her brother or sister and you said to them, "Tell them you're sorry!" Would you agree that the majority of the time they did not want to say, "I'm sorry?" Finally, with your kind and adamant, unbending persuasion, they say those words with a feeble, almost nonverbal voice of, "I'm sorry."

I have experienced this many times with our two daughters. Usually, it was the youngest who was the "little pest" to her big sister. Andrea wanted to be just like her older sister, Sherra. Even though she was almost five years younger, she could act and talk like a fifteen-year-old at the vibrant age of ten. She thought that she should be included in the interaction of Sherra and her teenage friends. And if she was not considered in the group sessions, she had a great number of offenses "up her sleeve."

It was not very long until I heard the irritated voice of my oldest daughter screaming, "You better stop it or I'm going to tell Mom."

Then I would hear, "Mom, Andrea won't leave us alone." After the slamming of doors and a few loud exchanges of not-so-sisterly words, I would proceed to put on my buttoned-at-the-collar referee shirt and enter the ring

The bell had rung and I had the mike! I was then the main attraction in the ring. When I got the whole story, with plenty witnesses around, I was told the whole truth and nothing but the truth. My sweet little, bouncy, vibrant ten-year-old had landed a right jab on her sister's upper body.

I grabbed Andrea by the hand and said to her, "Tell your sister you're sorry." Most of the time, Andrea's response was with her head down, and very softly, almost unheard, the words came out, "I'm sorry." If it was too faint, I would make her say it again, until it sounded like she could have possibly meant it. Then I would make her leave Sherra and her friends alone.

Here was my mistake. After Andrea said that she was sorry, I only dealt with her. I never turned to Sherra and taught her that she must forgive Andrea and then teach her how to forgive.

Did you ever realize that we more often put the emphasis on the child who has to repent than the child who has to forgive? We make sure that the one who has brought the offense knows that he/she must repent, but we leave the one who has been offended alone, taking for granted that they have forgiven or eventually will forgive the offense.

I can honestly say that I was guilty of this more than one time. And I would say that you probably were, too. There are a couple of reasons for this. One is because you and I never learned this lesson as a child when we were offended by our siblings. Our parents never taught us how to forgive because they were not taught how to forgive. It was like a generational cycle. But that cycle can be stopped with us.

The other reason for our ignorance concerning forgiveness is that we never learned from the church how to forgive. You must remember that the Lord can never accept either of these excuses as justification of our unforgiveness. He knows that for us to be forgiven by Him we must forgive others. The responsibility lies upon our shoulders. We have His Word and the Holy Spirit as our teacher.

THE STAMPEDE OF OFFENSE

Now, let's see what Jesus says about offense. Will you agree that offense seems to come to us like a stampede? It does not just walk up to us and tap us on the shoulder and say, "Excuse me, I am here to hurt you." NO! Offense comes running to us like it is going to knock us down and trample us under its feet. This is what the psalmist was talking about in Psalm 91:13. He basically said that those things that would come to destroy us, we can trample under our feet. So let's see how we can trample down offense and unforgiveness.

In Luke 17:1 the Lord is talking to His disciples and says, "It is impossible but that offenses will come: but woe unto him, through whom they come!" And in Matthew 18:7, Jesus says, "Woe unto the world because of offenses, for offenses must come. But woe unto that man by whom the offense comes!" The word *woe* here is an exclamation of grief.

Some critics have said that the Lord Jesus used this word when he expressed sympathy and concern. In other words, the Lord knows what is going to happen to the one who brings the offense. It means that suffering and grief are pronounced immediately on the one that brings the offense. God places a word of judgment first upon the offender. He then says they are going to have grief and suffering unless they repent!

Now, when someone offends us, our first thought is not

what is going to happen to him or her. Our thoughts are all about what is happening to us. We are hurt! We have been offended, abused, and taken advantage of.

If you will notice, the Lord does what we do when we deal with our children offending one another. He deals with the offender first. But the majority of the instruction given by our Lord is not to the offender. It is to the one to whom the offense has come.

Look again in this verse. Jesus says that it is a fact: you will have offenses come to you! You cannot stop them from coming. They are a part of the world system in which we live. And they will come because we are still in that imperfect state. So He says that they must come.

The word *offense* here means "a snare or a trap" (Thayer's). It is like the picture of a trapper preparing his trap for the prey. I am sure you have seen this scene before, where a box is made and one end of the box is elevated with a stick. The prey is lured into the trap with the bait, then the stick is triggered and the prey is caught. That is what offense is. It is a trap. And that trap is set with the bait of hurt, rejection, abuse, or some type of painful offense. It, like that trap, tempts us to enter, then it grabs hold of us!

All the while, we think that if we enter into the offense and take charge of it, somehow we can deal with it or figure out how to fix what needs to be fixed so that we will not hurt anymore. We think that we have the ability and strength to handle offense. But the Lord says that we are not to enter into the offense.

THE OFFENDER AND THE OFFENDED

When Jesus begins His instruction to His disciples concerning forgiveness, He says:

> It were better for him [the offender] that a millstone
> were hanged about his neck, and he cast into the sea,
> than that he should offend one of these little ones.
>
> —MATTHEW 18:6, AUTHOR'S PARAPHRASE

He is saying that it would be better for him to have died before he had ever committed the sin. And the reason for that was because of the reaping that he/she will receive because they brought the offense.

Now, that is a very strong statement made by our Lord. But the act of injuring the feeblest Christian or causing him to sin will be regarded by Christ as a most serious offence, and it will be punished accordingly.

The words, *it would be better* actually mean that the offender would profit only if he was to die before he hurts someone.[2] He has no reward except judgment and that with grief and suffering if he chooses not to repent.

Now remember, Jesus first speaks about the offender. Now, He is going to instruct the one who has been offended. He speaks: "Take heed to yourselves. If thy brother trespass against thee, rebuke him" (Luke 17:3). Figuratively speaking He says to "take hold of your mind; pay attention and grab hold of self."

Here it is. If your brother or sister sins against you, rebuke him or her. Now, you must know, and not from hearsay, that they have sinned against you. You cannot say, "I think he or she did this to me or I heard that he or she did this to me." But you must know that they have offended you. The offense most often should come directly to you.

Unfortunately, the majority of the time, you and I do not experience offense in this way in the ministry. So many times

[2] *Barnes' Notes*, Electronic Database. Copyright ©1997 by Biblesoft.

Satan is subtler in his approach because he does not want us to be able to see the instruction of the Lord and follow it. He does not want us to have the opportunity to rebuke because that will give the one who has offended us the opportunity to repent. He hates repentance! You see, for someone to be forgiven, there must be the opportunity to repent. Satan's job is to thwart repentance. His tactics are most often under the table.

Now, let's look. Jesus said, "If he repents, forgive him." How can such a little word like *if* hold such a big part in our response to life? Because *if* is a conditional participle; forgiveness toward the offender rests upon the condition of there being repentance.

I can see your mind working now. You are probably saying, "That's right. I don't have to forgive them until they repent." Well, you are partially correct, but do not take what Jesus is saying and add to or subtract from His words. He is saying that He wants the offender to be blessed with the opportunity to repent. And if they do not respond to that blessing of repentance, then the judgment of grief and suffering is their reward.

Then what are we to do if they do not repent? We are always to hold a forgiving heart toward them so that when they repent, they immediately receive true forgiveness from us. This is how our heavenly Father responded toward us when we were sinners.

He made it possible before the foundation of the world that Jesus was "the lamb that was slain" for our sin (Rev. 13:8). Even before we were born the Father made it possible for us to be forgiven of the sin nature that came in us at our birth. He has always carried the forgiving heart toward you and me. But you and I had to repent in order to receive the blessing of forgiveness.

Now, what is amazing is that Jesus did not stop there. He

proceeded to tell us that we were not just going to deal with one offense, but multiple offenses. "And if he trespass against thee seven times in a day, and seven times in a day turn again to thee, saying, I repent; thou shalt forgive him" (Luke 17:4).

He did not say anything about one offense being different from another. Your brother or sister could bring the same offense several times a day…seven to be exact. In Matthew 16:22, the Lord responded to Peter concerning his question about forgiveness. Peter asked if he had to forgive seven times. Jesus said that he had to forgive 490 times, or with every offense there must be the opportunity to repent and forgive.

You and I should not be surprised when people keep sinning in the same way, over and over again. The reason is that we only have three ways that we can sin. Here they are:

1. The lust of the flesh
2. The lust of the eyes
3. The pride of life

John wrote this:

> Love not the world, neither the things that are in the world. If any man love the world, the love of the Father is not in him. For all that is in the world, the lust of the flesh, and the lust of the eyes, and the pride of life, is not of the Father, but is of the world.
>
> —1 JOHN 2:15–16

It is only in these three ways will you and I or anyone else be tempted to sin. It is only through these three ways that offense will come.

Let's go back and see the instruction that we learned as children concerning forgiveness. Were you taught by your parents how to forgive someone? I was not. Neither was my mom or dad, and neither were their parents. It goes back to generations of the same. How can we know how to teach others to forgive if knowing how to forgive is something that we never learned?

If you have children, know this: they are watching your every move. They are looking at what you do with offense. It is just like anything else. If they do not learn from us how to deal with offenses, they will learn it from someone else. It is for sure that we do not want them to learn how to forgive like the world forgives!

What is the most important lesson to know about forgiveness is that Jesus said the only way for us to be forgiven is that you and I must forgive others. In the Gospels of Matthew, Mark, and Luke, we are told that our forgiveness rests upon our forgiving others of the offenses they bring to us. This means that we must carry a forgiving heart, always ready to receive the repentance from the offender.

HOW DO YOU FORGIVE A HYPOCRITE?

Most of the time, you are going to deal with those who say one thing but do another. All the while, they are smiling and speaking words of love and appreciation to your face. But after they leave, Mr. Hyde takes over and the same person who spoke those eloquent words about you is attacking your character. Is this what James was speaking about when he mentioned sweet and bitter water coming from the same fountain? (See James 3:9–10.)

Look at what Jesus says about how we are to treat people. In Luke 6:32–36 Jesus begins teaching his disciples what makes their love different from the love of the world's system. He says, "If you love those who love you, what credit is that to you? Even 'sinners' love those who love them."

Jesus is actually saying here is that when we love this way it really expresses a self-gratifying love. "He who loves for the sake of pleasure or interest, pays himself."[1] Why? Because it is not a genuine love for the character. But it is a love for the benefit. We love for what we benefit in the relationship. It makes us feel "real good" when we are loved back by people.

You see, it is a relationship that we have with people. It is either:

- A relationship of love.

- A relationship of no feeling, where you do not like them and you do not dislike them; perhaps you see them as just acquaintances.

- A relationship filled with disdain, intolerance, or even hate.

Jesus goes on to say:

> And if you do good to those who are good to you, what credit is that to you? Even "sinners" do that. And if you lend to those from whom you expect repayment, what credit is that to you? Even "sinners" lend to "sinners," expecting to be repaid in full.
>
> —LUKE 6:33–34, NIV

You see, the world loves those who love them, will do good to those who do good to them, and will lend to those who will pay them back.

But Jesus says that we, as His children, are not to be limited to that fleeting reward. We are to receive the reward that

[1] Adam Clarke, *Adam Clarke's Commentary* (Dallas, TX: Word Publishing, 1997).

comes from our heavenly Father, which is the "great" reward.

Verse 35 of Luke 6 continues with the words of Jesus. He says, "'But love your enemies, do good to them, and lend to them without expecting to get anything back.' 'Then,' says the Lord, 'your reward will be great, [much; far surpassed that which is expected; overly abundant; a surprise package from God, the Father] and you will be sons [not a child any longer, but a son with full rights of sonship] of the Most High'" (author's paraphrase).

He goes on to say that we have to do this because the Father is kind to the ungrateful and wicked. Verse 36 says, "Be merciful, just as your Father is merciful."

So Jesus says that even the world forgives. People who are not Christians forgive! What is the difference in how the world forgives and how the Christian forgives? Well, the major difference is that the world can be selective when it comes to forgiveness. People living by the world's standards can:

1. Forgive or not forgive.

2. Decide who they will forgive and who they will not forgive.

3. Forgive partially.

4. Act like they forgive without actually forgiving. In other words, they can lie about forgiving.

Their unforgiveness can hide in their dark spirit!

Because forgiveness is an act of the heart, they can never totally forgive! Why? It is because they are dead toward forgiveness.

Ephesians 2:1–3 says, "And you hath he quickened, who

were dead in trespasses and sins." The word *dead* means "dead." You see, Paul wrote to the church in Ephesus and stated that we were "dead in our trespasses and sins" before we came to Christ (Eph. 2:1).

So, what do you do when you are dead? Well, you only do those things that are found in death, for you are not alive to anything around you except death! And you do whatever death commands you to do.

In this case, you are dead in trespasses. *Trespasses* is "side-slipping; walking in error, offense, and transgression" (Strong's).

The word *sins* is translated as "unrighteousness; in violation of God's law; a wandering from God's way; offense" (Strong's). The key word is *in*. You are "in" death, so you do what death commands.

Verse two says, "Wherein in time past ye walked according to the course of this world, according to the prince of the power of the air, the spirit that now worketh in the children of disobedience." So in the spirit of disobedience resides unforgiveness.

Paul goes on to say in verse three, "Among whom also we all had our conversation in times past in the lusts of our flesh, fulfilling the desires of the flesh and of the mind; and were by nature the children of wrath, even as others."

He says that before we knew Jesus as our Savior:

- We walked in the conformity and mannerisms of death.

- We were lead by the devil.

- We were disobedient to everything outside of death.

- Our lifestyle was lived in the "cravings of death."

- We were full of wrath and even given the name of "child of violence; anger; and vengeance."

So, it doesn't matter how good you may be morally, or even how "polished" your actions may be. Paul wrote by the Holy Spirit to us and said, "If you do not have Jesus Christ in your heart…you are DEAD!"

Paul goes on to say in Colossians 2:13 (NIV), "When you were dead in your sins and in the uncircumcision of your sinful nature, God made you alive with Christ. He forgave us all our sins."

Peter wrote:

> He himself bore our sins in his body on the tree, so that we might die to sins and live for righteousness; by his wounds you have been healed. For you were like sheep going astray, but now you have returned to the Shepherd and Overseer of your souls.
> —1 PETER 2:24–25, NIV

Would you have to say that the reason that your enemy is your enemy is because at sometime in the relationship there was an offense? Or are you like the Hatfields and McCoys— and you just inherited an enemy! It does not matter how that enemy enters your life, the instruction from the Lord stands as written: We must forgive! So how do you forgive a hypocrite? You forgive them the same way Jesus forgives you—not on merit but by mercy.

FACING THE STAMPEDE OF OFFENSE, HEAD ON!

OK, so where do we start in walking in the obedience of forgiveness? Well, I am glad you asked.

First, it takes a born-again spirit that is reconciled to God by Jesus Christ in order for us to forgive the way we are commanded to forgive. That's right! We are commanded by the Lord Jesus to forgive!

Now, again, that may sound harsh. And the reason that it may sound harsh is because we have a tendency to categorize sin. We believe in God's eyes that adultery is worse than not forgiving someone who has hurt us. We feel that murder is worse than hatred.

The Holy Spirit thinks that sin is sin. He was so strong in that belief that He spoke to us through the pen of one of the greatest New Testament pastors, James, the pastor at Jerusalem. In James 4:17 (NIV) he wrote: "Anyone, then, who knows the good he ought to do and doesn't do it, sins." That little verse says a mouthful!

Even if you are a person who believes that one sin is worse to God than another, look what Solomon wrote about what God hates. In Proverbs 6:16-19 he says:

> There are six things the LORD hates, seven that are detestable to him: haughty eyes, a lying tongue, hands that shed innocent blood, a heart that devises wicked schemes, feet that are quick to rush into evil, a false witness who pours out lies.

Now, look at the seventh thing. "And a man who stirs up dissension among brothers" (NIV). The truth of the matter is that anyone who stirs up strife is full of unforgiveness. God says that is detestable to Him.

You and I have to remember that we are not saved necessarily for what we do. But we are saved from what we are. It is our sin nature that separates us from God, not the by-product of that nature.

In Matthew 6:14–15 (NIV) Jesus says, "For if you forgive

men when they sin against you, your heavenly Father will also forgive you. But if you do not forgive men their sins, your Father will not forgive your sins."

Do you read what I read in these scriptures? I think these scriptures say that in order for us to be forgiven, we have to forgive.

Would you agree that "out of sight, out of mind" is much easier to handle than when the stampede of offense is trying to run you over?

That's right! Offense comes like a stampede! And when the stampede of offense comes toward you, there is only one place to hide and be protected. And that is behind the rock, called Christ Jesus! He is your only protection!

It is for sure that you cannot outrun the stampede of offense. Neither can you charge back, to use a sports term, because you would be all alone! Jesus is your only defense, and we have to use the defensive weapons that come with Him!

If He is our defense and we are to use His weapons, what then does He say for us to do when we are facing the stampede of offense?

Before we answer this question, let's look at some offenses that might face us as pastors' and ministers' wives.

1. Let's say that you are a new pastor's wife at a new church.
   a. You are always being compared to the former pastor's wife.
   b. You are either shunned by some of the congregation or you are given no respect as the pastor's wife.

2. You befriended a woman in the church that had influence. You disagreed with her. She turned on

you and began turning the other ladies against you.

3. One of the elders is against your husband and he is beginning to sow discord very subtly among the people.

4. Some of the members' children have hurt your children. They have intentionally left them out and have said cruel words concerning them.

5. A staff member is disgruntled. They have been at the church longer than you.
   a. They rebel against your husband's instruction.
   b. They lay in wait to trap him in his words.
   c. They subtly get the other staff members involved in the discord.
   d. They are living in sin, but they have carefully hidden the physical proof of it. You just know by the Spirit of God that there is something wrong in their life.
   e. They lie with their words and it looks as if their words are truth in the ears of their hearers.

6. You see your husband make a mistake in the ministry. It brings division between the two of you. You refuse to forgive him because you are not at fault. Trust between the two of you is beginning to deplete.

7. You have prayed and asked God to intervene in a certain situation, and for some reason the answer did not come the way you expected, or it has not come even to this day. You are disillusioned with God and have anger in your heart toward Him, but you continue to hide it!

8. You made your children comply with rules of the church. When they got older, they rebelled, and now they will have nothing to do with the church. You blame the church for their waywardness.

9. You were abused as a child. What is worse is that it may have come through a relative or even a sinful church member. You have never dealt with it. And now everything in your life is affected because of that abuse.

You and I can look at these examples and truly say like the disciples said, "Lord, increase our faith." Surely, it takes a great deal of faith to forgive in any of these situations.

So, WWJD—or what would Jesus do?

Well, it is for sure that He would do what God's Word said to do. For He was the Word of God and He proved to us as a model of God's Word—that it is the only way to go.

So, look again in chapter seventeen of Luke. He is speaking to the disciples on how to forgive those who offend you. What is amazing to me is that Jesus used the illustration relating to a "brother that offends." For isn't it true that the pain of offense hurts the worse with those who are supposed to love us and be as close as family to us?

God's Word states:

> Then said he unto the disciples, It is impossible but that offences will come: but woe unto him, through whom they come! It were better for him that a millstone were hanged about his neck, and he cast into the sea, than that he should offend one of these little ones.
>
> —Luke 17:1–6

Remember that Jesus is showing His disciples an exclamation of grief, that those who would bring or carry the offense will experience a dreadful judgment! He says that it will be so "dreadful," compared to what they are going to experience (if they don't repent), that it would be better for him to die the death of shameful drowning in a sea. It would be better to go to a place where no one will ever remember him/her than ever to offend one of God's "little ones" by bringing a stumbling block that causes them to sin.

I believe the Lord gives this judgment in such a strong way so that the disciples will not fall into becoming the offender, themselves. For He says in verses two through six:

> Take heed to yourselves: if thy brother trespass against thee, rebuke him; and if he repent, forgive him. And if he trespass against thee seven times in a day, and seven times in a day turn again to thee, saying, I repent; thou shalt forgive him. And the apostles said unto the Lord, Increase our faith. And the Lord said, If ye had faith as a grain of mustard seed, ye might say unto this sycamine tree, Be thou plucked up by the root, and be thou planted in the sea; and it should obey you.

So, in simple steps, here is the Lord's way to forgive:

1. If you are offended and it is possible, rebuke in love directly to that person.

2. If he repents, forgive him by plucking up out of you any bitterness, resentment, anger that comes alongside of offense.

3. By the Holy Spirit, take your faith and cast that root of bitterness into the sea of forgetfulness.

This is where the Lord casts your sins and mine.

4. Because of the exercising of your faith, not the size, but the quality, bitterness must go and unforgiveness will not take root. This is the promise of the Holy Spirit.

5. Repeat steps one through four each time the offense is repeated. Be careful not to allow any offense to stay in your heart.

6. Continue to carry a forgiving heart so that when offense comes, whether the offender repents or not, you are standing absent of bitterness, and forgiveness is instant and continual. Remember, this is how the Lord's heart is set toward you and me when we offend Him.

This biblical formula is guaranteed. But it must be followed without deviation. And when you and I forgive those who offend us, the Lord promises His forgiveness toward us. And the "stampede of offense" will not trample us, for we will always be moving out of its way!

Chapter 10

When the Sheep Divide

But he that is an hireling, and not the shepherd, whose own the sheep are not, seeth the wolf coming, and leaveth the sheep, and fleeth: and the wolf catcheth them, and scattereth the sheep.

—JOHN 10:12

F I COULD rate the experiences that my husband and I have had in the ministry that brought hurt and pain, on the scale of 1–10, the experience of "the dividing of the sheep" would be a 15. It is true that life is full of painful experiences. But when you are called into the ministry, the situations that bring about hurt and tragedy escalate to a height that can only come through some type of wild imaginations. And only your enemy, the devil, has an imagination that can think up such horrific situations. And his goal is always to "catch and scatter."

In this chapter, I am going to give to you the most painful

experience of the "dividing of the sheep" that my husband and I have experienced. But by the Holy Spirit, you will be able to see how the Lord will bring you through the fire and how you can come out with not even the smell of smoke upon you.

That does not mean you will not remember the heat of the battle, nor will you ever forget the pain of the situation. And you will most likely experience some of the residue of being cast into the furnace. But your heavenly Father will make sure that you will not be destroyed when you follow His leading.

THE "WHY" OF DIVISION

Let me say this right up front: knowing the *why* of division does not help lessen the pain, nor does it help in the recovery toward forgiveness and repentance. Even if you become aware of the possibility that the sheep may divide and you find out the cause of the division, you are not guaranteed that separation will not happen. You most likely cannot fix the why of the separation because it has gone too far, which makes it inevitable.

When our girls were growing up, they always wanted to know "why" I said they could not do something they wanted to do. Most of the time, when they asked why I said "No," they were really looking for a way to debate my ruling and possibly get their own way. But even when I would tell them "why," the pain of not being able to get their way was not at all lessened. In fact, sometimes it made them feel worse because the ruling of the "why" of the decision brought with it a finality.

Have you ever asked the Lord "why" when it comes to the sheep dividing? Are you in that position right now? My dear shepherd's wife, knowing the reason for something happening does not always fix the problem, especially when it comes to the evil deeds of carnality. There is not a rational explanation for division, except that it comes from the pit of hell, and it is orchestrated by your enemy, the devil.

Remember, it is the devil that brings division. He is the instigator. He first divided Eve from God when he told her that God was not being upfront with her. He insinuated that the Lord was keeping His best from her. And in her complete state of perfection, she believed the word of her enemy. How in the world could we believe that in our imperfection we are much more apt to handle deception? If she was perfect and believed a lie, where does that leave us?

One of the things I noticed about Eve is that she never confronted God with what the serpent had said to her. She just took the word of the enemy over the Word of the Lord.

It is not wrong for you and me to come to our heavenly Father and ask Him why. Now, grant you, He may not give you the answer you are looking for, but He will assure you that having His wisdom is what matters. And that wisdom is yours for the asking.

I know for sure that He will say to you that you must walk in His love toward your enemies. Your feelings of anger, resentment, and lashing back must be laid down at the feet of your Savior. Any reaction outside of our operating in His love will cause us to fail.

He will also tell you that His Spirit to overcome any obstacle is with you and in you. For the Lord of Host says, "It is not by might, nor by power, but by His Spirit" (Zech. 4:6). He will take care of you, your husband, your family, and the flock. And it is for certain, He will also take care of your enemy.

ARE YOU A HIRELING OR A SHEPHERD?

You have to remember that the herd of sheep in your care belongs totally to the Lord, and you and I are simply undershepherds. Just make sure that you are not a hireling. You may be thinking, "What is a hireling?" A *hireling* is someone who is only pastoring for the money or the glamour of the pastorate. Did I say glamour? Yes, there is a false sense of glamour in the ministry, and it comes by way of our flesh. And a hireling is full of the flesh!

A hireling does not really care what happens to the sheep. For when the wolf comes to prance upon the sheep, the hireling is afraid the wolf will turn and prance upon him. And rest assured, at that point, money is not an issue. There are jobs for hire out there that have much less stress, and they are a lot safer and sometimes even pay more money. To a hireling, his life is the main focus. It is all about HIM!

Also, in the case of a hireling, the sheep are not worth the fight. He does not like the ones who are contrary and bite and fight with him while he is on the job. He thinks those sheep deserve the attack of the wolf.

The hireling gives no warning to the sheep that the wolf is coming. He just runs for his life. To him nothing is lost, no matter how many sheep are destroyed; for they are not his anyway. He is only paid to try to keep them together. But, in his eyes, no sheep is worth fighting the wolf over.

On the other hand, a shepherd (or should I say, "under-shepherd") has the same heart as the Chief Shepherd He cares for the safety and maturity of the flock. He wants them to grow and multiply. The true shepherd watches out for the "little lambs." He makes sure they do not wander off from the flock and they are fed and taught so they will grow into healthy, happy adult sheep.

The shepherd expresses love to the lovable and unlovable sheep. He hurts when the carnal sheep bite one another, and he makes sure they are disciplined in the love of God. He does not leave them alone. Sometimes he separates them from the other sheep with his staff. But that is only until they learn to be kind to one another and not try to devour one another.

Sometimes the sheep turn and bite the shepherd and his family. And they may try to get other sheep to join in the attack. But the shepherd uses the wisdom of God and does not strike them in order to destroy them, but disciplines them so that they will see their wrongdoing and repent and turn from the evil deeds. If he does not walk in the love of God and operate in the wisdom of God concerning those unruly sheep; the blow that he will give in his anger and frustration could be the fatal blow. They might not recover.

It is like the old saying, "You can shear a sheep many times, but you can only skin them once!" If we as shepherds take our anger out on those contrary sheep, not caring about their eternal souls, then we have not done a shearing on them to discipline them. We have actually skinned them.

The true shepherd sees the wolf coming and prepares for the fight. He does not fight the sheep. Even when the sheep are unaware that the wolf is lurking in the darkness, the shepherd is watching and praying. For watching and praying is his defense. The Chief Shepherd will make sure that His under-shepherd is aware of the devices of the wolf. And by His Word and through prayer, the Lord will reveal the strategy of the war. That is when miracles will begin to happen in the flock. And the feeling of safety will be provided to you and the flock.

To be a shepherd is to be blessed. To be a hireling is to be miserable. That is not to say that a shepherd will not be miserable, for there is always the possibility of becoming "weary in well doing" (Gal 6:9). But the Scripture says that if we "do not faint," we will reap the rewards of the victory. The word *faint* in the Greek means to have one's strength relaxed, to become weary and tired out through exhaustion (Thayer's).

Allow me to give you another sidebar here. Do not allow yourself to get exhausted in the ministry! For exhaustion brings about burnout. And when you and I experience burnout we are miserable, to say the least.

The Lord says that our reward is His reward if we do not faint. And that reward is the harvest of souls. With His reward comes peace and rest. Make sure that you and your husband rest your bodies while you are pastoring. The enemy will tell you that is impossible, but again, he is a liar!

For the true shepherd, the reason for ministry is the harvest of souls. A shepherd wants everyone to go to heaven because He has the same passion that the Lord has: "That none should perish, but that all should come to repentance" (2 Pet. 3:9). Heaven is where the shepherd is leading the sheep. Even for those sheep who have acted like they do not deserve heaven, the shepherd is leading them there, also. You and your husband have seen by the Spirit a glimpse of hell. And there is no sheep, no matter how mean or carnal, that deserves the eternal separation that hell brings.

DEGREES OF DIVISION

Division comes in measurable degrees. You have small divisions that come between sheep. Those are like the "little spats" that your children have with each other. They may get angry with one another, but in a few hours, they are playing together again and have forgotten that there was even an argument.

Then you have those "bites" that are a little deeper and give a lasting imprint. That mark of division is not only visible to the ones who have been bitten, but also to those who may be standing around. And be assured of this one thing. The ones who have been bitten want everyone to see the bite. They will instantly become a martyr. And they will begin to get as many as they can to feel sorry for them and join them in their pain.

The attention from their martyrdom seems to fulfill any void that they have in their life, and they enjoy the sympathy. They keep stirring the pot as long as they can. And if that sheep who has been hurt is an expert at manipulation, you can have a serious problem on your hands. In every case, the Lord is your help because you have His wisdom in knowing how to rebuke and correct.

You see, the Lord sees the whole picture. He knows every motive that is behind all division. He knows the "how and the why" of manipulation, and He is also able to defuse any discord.

Just remember that you and your husband are not promised that there will be no pain in the correction. It is inevitable that there will be hurt and pain, and possibly, a separation of the sheep. But the seed of division is what you want to pluck up so that it cannot spread over the flock. One thing is for sure; you cannot caudle carnality or rebellion.

Remember what the Word of God says about rebellion? It is the same as witchcraft. And stubbornness is the same as idolatry. (See 1 Samuel 15:23.) These are works of the flesh, according to Galatians, chapter 5, and they cannot be dealt with lightly. But they must be dealt with in the wisdom of God and with the mercy of God! Every situation will have a different level of wisdom that is needed for correction.

So, you and your husband must hear from the Lord in the matter of dealing with rebellion and stubbornness. And I promise you, if your heart is fixed on the Lord, and you ask Him in faith, and you wait for His answer, He will come with His wisdom, and He will bring that wisdom to you liberally (James 1:5)!

Sometimes it may be difficult for you to know exactly what correction is necessary in dealing with carnality. And if that is the case, it is better to err on the side of mercy than to follow through with some type of discipline that is processed through human wisdom.

You have to wait and listen in order to know how to follow the Lord's instruction. For the flock really is His, and He knows how to correct His children.

THE WOLF IN SHEEP'S CLOTHING

The most devastating degree of division is done through the person who is really a wolf, but all dressed up in sheep's clothing. Here is what God's Word has to say about it:

> Beware of false prophets, which come to you in sheep's clothing, but inwardly they are ravening wolves.
> —MATTHEW 7:15

The New Living Translation says:

> Beware of false prophets who come disguised as harmless sheep, but are really wolves that will tear you apart. You can detect them by the way they act, just as you can identify a tree by its fruit.
> —MATTHEW 7:15–16, NLT

The words *false prophet* are translated in other versions as "false teachers." *Strong's Concordance* says that the Greek word means "religious imposter."

Every Christian is a carrier of the gospel for we are all commissioned by the Lord to spread His Good News. But a false prophet or a religious imposter is anyone who professes Christianity, but the fruit of Christ is not present in his life.

173

Now, they disguise themselves with fruit that looks like the fruit of the Spirit. But in actuality, they are like artificial and plastic fruit. And you cannot tell from a distance if they are real or not. You have to get closer in order to recognize what is false and what is real.

Today, manufacturers are producing artificial fruit in such a way that even the touch of the fruit feels real. I know from experience. I picked up an apple that looked like the most delicious, red Washington. It felt real. It looked perfect. And I like fruit with no bruises or imperfections. Then I tried to take a bite and realized that it was made from some type of rubber product. How disappointing! I was really fooled by not only how it looked, but also how it felt. It was only when I tried to take a bite that I realized I had been fooled into believing that the apple was actually real. The result of biting the fake fruit was that I almost lost one of my front teeth.

You must be careful as shepherds. For when the wolf in sheep's clothing is revealed to you and your husband, great danger is lurking for you and the flock. The reason for this is that wolves cannot lose their disguise prematurely. If they do, they will be revealed as rapacious and insatiable carnivores, not sparing the flock. Remember, they do not care what happens to the sheep.

All that is important to them is that they are not exposed. For in not being exposed as a wolf, they have a greater opportunity to destroy more sheep. If they are exposed, they become outwardly vicious and destroy whoever gets in their way. And the greater the destruction, the greater their satisfaction!

FIGHTING THE REAL DIVIDER

I must tell you that I believe the Bible literally, when it says that our battle is not with flesh and blood:

> For we wrestle not against flesh and blood, but against
> principalities, against powers, against the rulers of the
> darkness of this world, against spiritual wickedness in
> high places.
>
> —EPHESIANS 6:12

That means that no human being is the root source of the
evil that is coming against us. It is orchestrated from the spiritual wickedness in the heavenly realm.

Personally, I believe that Paul is telling us that principalities, or high ruling demonic powers, and princes of evil
(including Satan, himself) are set over cities, provinces, and
nations of the world. They are set there to execute the sinful darkness that comes from the prince of darkness himself,
namely, Satan.

Their whole goal is to derail, stop, and even destroy any
likeness of the kingdom of God, which might come and per-
meate the people of that city or nation. And they use their
weapons of mass destruction upon mankind. For their sole
purpose is to steal, kill, and destroy!

Now, hear this! Anyone is susceptible to their attack. But
their highest goal is to go for the flock of God, and most
importantly, the leadership, and bring destruction so that the
sinner will not see any difference between the church and the
world. And ultimately, the sinners will not consider Jesus as
being the Savior of the world, because they will not be able to
see Him in the church.

These demonic rulers will always run after the leadership
of the church. And they do not hold anything back when it
comes to destroying them, their families, or their influence
with the flock. They feel that the destruction of the leadership
brings the greatest devastation to the kingdom of God.

For, it is the leadership that is to exemplify the power of

the love of God. And it is from the leadership that the world should see the goodness and kindness of the heavenly Father. If the leadership falls, the domino effect begins. And innocent little lambs are always affected, and some are even destroyed.

In our particular case, we were sent to a town where the ruling principality was two-fold. There was a spirit of Jezebel that seemed to rule over the town. For those of you who are reading this book and you have never heard anyone speak about "spiritual warfare," let me explain what I mean by the spirit of Jezebel.

When you look in the Old Testament and you see the woman called Jezebel, you see an evil woman in the history of Israel. She was full of witchcraft and she used manipulation to express her evil, domineering character. She was a murderer and a seducer and no one was to confront her evil without great consequence. Everyone was afraid of what she might do if she got angry.

This is what I mean by the spirit of Jezebel operating in a town. There will be rebellion, division, witchcraft, and manipulation. This spirit can reside within the government of the town, in businesses, in schools, and even in families. But where it is the most destructive is when it finds a home in the church.

When we first moved into our town, I wanted to have a luncheon for the local pastors' wives. So I organized my women's group and asked them to contact each of the churches and the pastor's wife for each. There were several little communities surrounding our town, so I gave two of the ladies the task of taking care of only our town. I told them to contact only the churches that preached the death, burial, and resurrection of Jesus. I told them not to contact any cults or churches that did not teach that Jesus was the Son of God and Savior.

To my surprise they came back with 119 different churches in our little town, alone. I was shocked. The first thing that came to my mind was, "Wow, what great division!" Later, I found out that a great majority of those churches came by way of split after split after split! So there was a great spirit of division that ruled over the city and it had filtered into the churches.

There was also a spirit of adultery that brought in a spirit of perversion. I had never experienced so many divorced families in all my life. And what was sad was that a great majority of the marriages that had stayed in tact were miserable marriages. Some of the couples had even voiced having lustful desires for someone other than their own spouse. They treated the marriage vow as no more than the "going steady" commitment. They rationalized within themselves that marriage meant living with someone until you found someone that you liked better.

The church had battled with perversion and rebellion for years. Many of the battles were not won with victory over ungodly desires. And the saddest of all was that the children of the families reaped the consequences.

When a spirit of Jezebel rules in a church, no one seems to be concerned about the children. For with this spirit comes the demand that says, "My desires must be satisfied!" The "Me, My, Mine, and I" syndrome is what matters, because selfishness is the major characteristic of this spirit. And selfishness was running rampant! But God loved all of the sheep and wanted them to repent and change, for He knew the devastation that was ahead for them. And what they would reap would be greater than they could bear.

When we, as human beings, operate in our own will and our own desires discounting God's will and His desires, we reap a whirlwind of pain and hurt. Getting our own way will always bring temporary satisfaction and with it comes unending selfishness and an unfulfilled life. This selfishness brings with it separation, loneliness, division, jealousy, suspicion, and great heartache.

THE PAINFUL DIVISION

The stirring of rebellion was deeply rooted in some of the leadership of the church. And when people operate in rebellion against authority, they never want to take responsibility for wrongdoing on their part. Someone else is always to blame.

This precious church had been infiltrated by the enemy with a great spirit of rebellion. This was definitely the major sin in the camp. Yet my husband was instructed by the Lord to walk in humility and respond with mercy. He began giving, unconditionally, especially to the staff of the church.

I know that some of them had never experienced this before because they did not know how to receive someone loving them without an ulterior motive. That is what comes with the spirit of Jezebel. There is always a spirit of suspicion and fear. And for those who have attached themselves with that spirit, they will walk around like someone has a private agenda against them. It was not revealed until later that it was them, personally, who had the private agenda.

Those operating in that spirit really did not want my husband and me to come as pastors of the church. So we were marked before we ever went. But our appointment came from the Lord. He is the one who destined us to go. And I know that it would not have mattered who came as pastor; at some point, they would still be unhappy.

When you look at people's lives and you see what pain

that they are going through, sometimes you can understand why they are fighting you so hard. They want everyone to hurt like they are hurting, especially those who seem to be happy in living a Christian life.

Understanding that in their own personal lives they had experienced so much pain helped me and my husband to continue to be kind and good to them. Although, to this day, some of them will never admit that we were ever good to them.

In the first three weeks of pastoring, my husband was bombarded with information that was unbelievable. He was told of past infidelities, improprieties, and sexual perversion that would cause any new pastor to run. But the Lord had placed us in that pastorate. No man was responsible for us going to that church. It was a "God thing!"

I wish that I was with you while you were reading this book so that I could express to you in person how through all of the rejection that was directed toward us, we still loved those who were fighting against us. But for some reason beyond our control, they would not receive love from us.

The rebellion and strategic plans to impeach my husband continued. There would be statements made like, "He's not the same man in the pulpit when he's out of the pulpit." Well, to a certain extent that was correct. His position, for instance, to the staff was two-fold. He was not only their pastor but also their employer. And as their employer, he was supposed to be able to give a directive concerning the administration of the church and they were to follow through. But that was not always the case.

Sometimes in the early days of this pastorate, he would not be informed of people who had died in the church. He would hear about it maybe a day or sometimes two days later so that he would not be able to minister to the family. They wanted him to be portrayed to the congregation as "the noncaring pastor." When he would have to discipline or correct a staff member for doing something that would inevitably hurt the sheep, they would become furious, inwardly, and sow seeds of discord among themselves in order to discredit his ministry.

My husband would spend hours at a time, trying to think out how the problems with the division between him and staff could be rectified. We continued to pray and fast and walk in the love of the Lord even when that was refuted by the staff. And I cannot tell you how many times I saw the Lord give to the staff opportunity after opportunity to experience the freedom that comes when we make the choice to not live a rebellious life. It is a life of submission, that always brings an inward peace.

My husband never did or never would ask them to do anything that would harm or degrade them as people. It would be just small directives for the operation of the ministry that he would ask them to do. But the motivation behind either ignoring or simply just not following through with those directives was far deeper than any surface feelings. There was great disdain and hatred for my husband and me. And it accelerated as the congregation began to love us and receive the preached Word.

Rebellion is so ugly. And it brings so much hurt and pain. And no one benefits from it. It only destroys and divides. And Satan just sits and laughs because the little lambs begin to scatter. Remember, He is the enemy not the people who have submitted to the rebellion.

After three years of this pressure, day and night, my husband began to have severe chest pains. He went for a checkup and the doctor ordered a stress test. The diagnosis was four blockages, so he was immediately scheduled for open-heart surgery.

Can I tell you that my husband's main concern through-out the entire procedure was, "Who is going to care for the people?" He knew the discord against him was coming from a staff in which some of them did not know how to care for the sheep. And those who did know the principles of ministry either relaxed or set themselves up as "the minister." Their goal was to see us fail. And again, all of this was orchestrated from the principalities that ruled in the heavenlies. All that the enemy needed was a "willing vessel" who might have held on to some past hurts and pain in their life that had caused them to be bitter. Bitterness will always bring about evil plots. And remember this, no one is exempt from the devil's schemes!

And I can say again, anyone is susceptible. No one is exempt from the temptation to be bitter. But you and I have to make the choice to walk in love and stand if no one is standing with us. In the ministry, a great many times, it is only you and the Lord standing together!

If we had retaliated with carnal weapons to try to destroy those who were trying to destroy us, we would have lost! But we chose not to expose to destroy. And even though it appeared to some and was reported that past sins were exposed in order to destroy, that was just another lie from the enemy. You see, when someone wants to follow through with an evil plot, there must be an explanation in their defense of why they do what they do. And be assured, they personally will not be the ones to blame.

In our case, after those who were angry and upset at my husband had split from our church, we found out that they had been planning to leave and start a church for several months. But we did not retaliate!

Remember this: if you as a shepherd try to expose a sin or wrongdoing of one of your sheep, staff, or leadership in order to destroy their credibility, you will not be vindicated by the Lord. You never expose to destroy for that puts you on the same level of those who are trying to destroy you. And you will never win that way!

My husband stood for the staff when he did not have to. When some of the congregation and even other leadership in the church wanted to destroy a certain staff member and his family because they just did not like them, J. D. stopped it because their motive was to destroy.

One member wanted to destroy a staff member because of past indiscretions. But my husband would not allow that member to do it. And the staff person even asked J. D. if he wanted him and his family to leave and go work somewhere else. J. D.'s response was, "No! You have told me that repentance and discipline were given years ago. And as far as I'm concerned, what the Lord forgives is forgiven." But J. D. continued by telling the staff person, "If this becomes a problem in the church, I will have to tell the elders and deal with it with them." The staff person agreed with him until it became a problem and J. D. had to deal with it with the elders. Then J. D. became the mean, unforgiving, evil pastor in his eyes and all of those who followed.

WHEN THE LORD DIVIDES

I will never forget that day. It was two days before Christmas that hell made a visit to the church. My precious husband had been taken to the hospital on the Thursday night before that dark Sunday morning. The staff had finalized their coalition and their army of disgruntled members to try to overthrow J. D. and the present leadership of the church.

Because he had just gotten out of the hospital late on Saturday afternoon, J. D. was too weak to make both morning worship services, so we waited to come to the 10:30 a.m. service.

When we arrived at the church, we were greeted with the news that no music was provided for the first service and the choir had retired to the balcony. A great majority of them did not really understand what was happening. All they had heard was that the some of the staff had been treated wrongly by the pastor.

My husband told me to lead in a couple of Christmas carols, and then he would address the congregation. He was too weak to preach that morning so he was just going to speak to the congregation and encourage them.

That morning the entire choir, except for four people, walked out while he was praying. The music pastor, his family and all of the music team left. The children's pastor and the children's workers left. About three weeks later, the youth pastor and the youth workers left. And then the pastoral care pastor left and carried with him many of the care workers.

You talk about devastation. And the hard thing was that my husband instructed the elders that they were not to respond negatively or in a degrading way toward those who left. That was the hardest thing to do. It seemed like that there was no opportunity to defend ourselves. We had been portrayed as destructive, evil people—people with no mercy or compassion.

Within the next few weeks and months the pain seemed to grow. We began to get threatening phone calls at home and messages left on our answering machine. Things like, "You better watch your back. I know when you are alone at the church. I know where you live! I'm going to see to it that you and your family hurt just like you hurt those fine staff people."

Then one morning I went outside to start my car and the ignition would not turn over. Fear like I had never experienced gripped my heart. I ran into the house and began to shake and cry. I yelled for J. D. to go outside and check underneath the hood of my car to make sure that there was not a bomb set to explode.

It was at that point that I began to pray with an urgency like I had never prayed before. My prayer was that God would deliver me from the fear of angry people. Immediately, and I mean immediately, His Holy Spirit began to comfort me and calm my heart.

I know that mistakes and wrong decisions will happen in the ministry to cause people to become angry and disagreeable. Never will I be ignorant in believing that we are not going to make mistakes and have failures while pastoring. Misunderstandings, hurts, wrong decisions, and even right decisions but in the wrong timing, will happen during a pastorate. But God knew the motive of our heart. It had never been nor would it ever be to damage or destroy anyone. But all of the blame for taking a stand for what was right focused toward my husband and myself.

We began to hear comments like, "How could four associate pastors be wrong? How could all of them be wrong? Surely, one of them would have stayed if everything was what it was supposed to be."

Taking that perspective into consideration, let's look at the twelve spies that were sent to Canaan to spy out the land. Of the twelve, ten were wrong in their viewpoint and only two were right.

And what about the scene in the Book of Acts? How could an entire church stone Stephen simply because He had preached the gospel, yet they declared him evil?

As the weeks passed, the pain of separation grew stronger and stronger. I watched my precious husband battle through rejection from people that he loved like his own family. I watched him go to the pulpit, Sunday after Sunday, broken, but never allowing the congregation to sense the deep grief that he was carrying. I sat amazed at the grace of God and how the Lord would touch him and anoint him to minister to those who had remained. I can tell you that God's grace was so amazing! Because J. D. had made the choice to minister to the congregation and allowed the Lord to heal his pain, the Holy Spirit was able to move and encourage and uplift the people even in his discouragement.

You see, there were people in the congregation that were hurting in their marriage, having trouble in their families and with their children, experiencing major health problems, death of loved ones; financial problems that were heading them towards bankruptcy, and so on. And they had come to church to get into the presence of the Lord and hear His Word in order to be strengthened. So our personal troubles had to be laid down for three to four hours, and the ministry of our Lord had to be the focus.

As for me, my prayers seemed to be nothing but grief. I had cried so much in my prayer time that I did not want to pray anymore. It seemed like all I could do was cry out to the Lord with excruciating sorrow. Until one day, the Lord jolted me with these words. He said to me, "I allowed this!"

Can I tell you that He got my attention! I knew His voice. That is why it took me by surprise. Then somehow my grieving prayer was laid aside because I had to have more from Him than just the words, "I allowed this"!

I began to question the Lord and say, "What do you mean, Lord? You are not the Lord of division. You want unity and harmony in your church." He answered me with, "Yes, I do want unity and harmony among my people, but that was not going to happen until there was a 'cutting away.'"

He immediately took me to the scriptures in Numbers 16 when the earth opened up and Korah and everything that appertained to him was swallowed up. The Holy Spirit began to instruct me on only the things about the dividing that He wanted me to know. He said that the dividing had to be great so that no residue of rebellion would spread through the congregation and destroy the seed for the vision for souls.

You see, it was not a matter of disagreement in administration. It was not even a dislike of the procedure that my husband and I had in executing the vision of ministry. It was all about rebellion. And the vision for souls will always be lost in rebellion. Your focus is not on winning souls to Christ. It is on getting your own way and doing your own thing.

Now, believe me. When the Lord spoke those words to me, it did not cause the pain of the separation to subside. I did not have the luxury to rationalize my position as being the victim of an undeserved tragedy. For the Lord's continual instruction to me was that I must walk in his love and that I must forgive, daily! And that was the hardest instruction from the Lord that I had ever received.

How was I supposed to love and forgive people that hated my husband to the point of harming him? How was I to be kind to those people who wanted to believe a lie? How do you smile and be nice to someone who has said they would rather "spend a week in hell, than ever work for your husband one day?" Evidently, they had no concept of what hell afforded for them.

Adding to the trauma, the separation not only affected our church, but also some of the pastors in our town who had fellowshiped with us; they became aloof. Because we would not blast out to them the garbage of what had happened, we were marked off. But the Lord was faithful and revealed friends in the ministry who loved us and supported us because we did not try to destroy and damage those who left. Gossip, whether true or false, is a horrible sin.

HEALING IN THE DIVISION

How did we pull through? Well, it was only by the mercy and grace of the Lord. It was only in our daily walk in the love of God and His forgiveness that we survived the evil devices and schemes of the enemy.

Remember, the only way for us to be forgiven is if you and I choose to forgive others. There is no other way. Know this: forgiveness is supernatural. We cannot forgive in our natural self, no matter how nice, or sweet, or kind, or good that we think we are. Goodness has no bearing on forgiveness.

You could sit down and take a pen and paper and write down all of the "good" that you have done and compare your good to their evil. All of that would be futile. Comparisons will never be accepted as a reason to not forgive.

You see, no one is good except the heavenly Father, according to Jesus. (See Matthew 19:17.) So it takes His Holy Spirit in you to actually bring about the forgiveness. Your part is to make the decision to forgive because forgiveness is a choice.

Choosing to forgive does not rid you of the pain of separation. But it does allow the Holy Spirit to heal your heart with His love so bitterness will not take root in you. Bitterness is such bondage.

I encourage you to pluck out any root of bitterness today with the Word of the Lord. The Lord says that He has given to us the faith to do it. (See Luke 17:1–6.) But you have to wake up every morning and decide, "Today, I am going to walk in the love of God and forgiveness." It is your choice!

How did things turn out? Well, we as a congregation (again only by the grace of the Lord) erected a first-phase, 45,000-square-foot sanctuary and worship center dedicated to the preaching and teaching of the gospel. Many families were won to the Lord, and the vision for souls became greater than ever before.

Because we continued to walk in forgiveness, the Lord had reconciled us with several of those families who had left. Some had come back to the church. But some did not, and that is OK.

You have to understand that when the enemy causes a division that is directed toward you and your husband, it becomes very difficult for those who stood against your leadership to receive the Word of God from your husband as their shepherd. They have been deceived by the enemy, the devil, to the point that what your husband would say, even concerning the Word of God, has no validity for them because confidence and trust in him as their shepherd is lost.

And sometimes, even though forgiveness has taken place between you and them, the relationship of pastor and member may never be restored. They may have to attend somewhere else in order to receive the Word of God and heal. And you have to let them go! For the greater purpose is that we continue to walk in the love of the Lord toward each other and go to heaven together.

As for me, the shepherd's wife, I can genuinely say that the Lord has taught me how to love like He does. And through that division, I realized that I really did not know how to love with God's love. But without reservation, I can say that I truly love all those who left. Only God could do that in me. But I had to make the choice on a daily basis to forgive and not offend.

When I would see them in the town, my mind would yell down to my heart and say, "Hey, there is the one who sided against your husband being pastor." And my heart would respond back to my mind, "Sorry, I do not know what you are talking about! There is no recollection of bitterness here. It must have been plucked out and cast into the sea."

Sometimes, my husband and I long to run to those who have left and hug them and tell them how much we love them, for they are not our enemy nor were they ever the enemy! Our enemy is not flesh and blood. Only when we choose to forgive will the Holy Spirit work that miracle in us.

Precious pastor's wife, there is life after division, but it is only through forgiveness!

Chapter 11

Growing Old With the Shepherd

*W*HEN I WAS a teenager, I used to think that anyone that was married for five years or more
was an old married couple. Then when I was
married for five years, I thought that couples who made it
to their twenty-fifth anniversary were really old, that is until
I reached my thirtieth year and I began to say, "How could
those years fly by so fast?"

J. D. and I have now been married for thirty-four years.
We have more years of marriage behind us than possibly
before us. But I can say without reservation, "God has been
good to me in giving me the perfect 'soul-mate.'" We are
so different, but we have complimented each other these
past thirty-four years. Where one was weak, the other was
strong. And the Lord has used this union to further His

kingdom, even with all of our failures and weaknesses.

It has been far from the perfect marriage. But our goal has always been to work at having a marriage that would grow in love toward the Lord and toward each other. The prayer I prayed most often was that I would not grow old and look back to only realize that I had not developed a relationship with the man that I had married.

So as I prayed that prayer the Lord began to give to me the instruction on how to be the "good wife" of my husband's youth. I did not always pass the test because those areas of weakness in my life seemed to be so monumental. I seemed to miss the mark more than hit the bull's eye! But God was faithful. He showed me how to not deviate from His path of instruction for marriage. And so that is what I did.

MARRIED AT EIGHTEEN AND INNOCENTLY HAPPY

In the first chapter of this book, you saw the beginning of not only our married life, but also the beginning of our life in ministry. We had to experience two major areas of life at the same time. And I can tell you for a fact that takes God to work, in order for survival to take place!

We began our union of marriage and ministry in an area of the country that was away from friends and family. That was one great plus for both of us. We had to work out our marriage just like we worked out our salvation, with fear and trembling. What was a married couple to do? Neither one of us had been married, so it was a brand new adventure.

Our only models were our parents, but that would only go so far with us because neither set of parents were in the ministry. So, I prayed and watched! I felt so vulnerable and sometimes alone in what to do, so I looked at other pastors' wives and saw the example they portrayed.

191

It was with careful, intent gazing at those marriages that the Lord helped me to see positive and negative aspects of marriage; things to do and not to do; ways to approach my mate and issues that just needed to be left alone or dropped.

Let me start by giving some of the negative observations first because I always like ending up on a positive note. It was these observations that I saw in the life of other ministers' wives that I did not want to happen in my marriage.

1. I did not like to hear a woman talk down about her husband in public or even to me or another friend. It really caused her to be somewhat degrading in my eyes. I thought, "What would he do if he knew what she was saying about him?"

2. I did not like how some of the middle-aged women portrayed their relationship with their husbands to others. A few of the pastors' wives that I watched at that time were in their forties to mid-fifties. They expressed no outward, loving relationship with their husband. In fact, some of them did not even seem to like their husbands. I noticed the harsh looks and the nonresponsive expressions given to their husbands while in public. And I could neither understand them nor accept them.

Grant you, as I matured in marriage and ministry I became more aware of how trust can be hindered or even broken in certain situations of life. But you and I do not have the luxury to allow bitterness, distrust, or feelings of hurt and pain to rule in our heart! We also do not have the luxury to express those feelings in our actions and countenance toward our friends, family members, or the congregation.

The Lord requires us, as His children, to forgive and to allow Him to heal our hearts from the pain of being mistreated in any way by others or our spouses. For it is sure, we are going to have tribulation (pressure, distress, affliction), but Jesus said that because He overcame the world, we are able to overcome, no matter how we feel! (See John 16:33.)

It was the apostle Paul who wrote that he was "persuaded" that when certain things would come into his life for the sole purpose to separate him from the love of Christ, they could not do it. (See Romans 8:38.) And when he used the word *persuaded*, he meant that he was "convinced and believed with a great conviction" that nothing could separate him from that love.

Persuaded is the key word. And how could he possess that word in his heart unless he had experienced those things and found that God's love was greater than the trouble. And he, through Christ, was able to hold to that love and let go of the hurt, pain, abuse, and rejection that he dealt with on a daily basis. Paul is giving us the answer, not only by revelation, but also by experience.

This is a fact. At some point in your marriage, your spouse is going to hurt you or disappoint you. It may be intentionally or unintentionally; that does not matter. But your response to that hurt can affect you for years if you do not deal with it. The pain has to be dealt with. It will not just "go away" without some resolution in your heart. What happens when we do not deal with pain and hurt is that it just keeps piling up and piling up.

The resolution happens inside of you, not in your spouse. The obligation lies with you and the Lord. You have to allow the Holy Spirit to convict you of any hurt that might have turned into bitterness and remove it, according to Luke 17. He promises that if you do that by faith, the root of bitterness has to come out and go to the sea! It all happens by faith. And it must be a daily faith that is operating.

Allow me to give you one more negative action that I saw in older pastors' wives that I did not want to happen in my life.

3. Because of the failed relationship between the pastor and his wife, I saw the wife latch on with an inordinate relationship toward their children. This all came about because of the failed marriage relationship. For one reason or another, the marriage relationship had stopped growing. And when that happened, those women began a relationship with their children that brought about an inordinate dependence of the mother to the child.

In other words, the mother's whole life was wrapped around her children. Her happiness and fulfillment in life revolved around them. And when the children grew up and left home, the wife was devastated. And in some cases, that devastation was so great that it resulted in divorce or it simply became a "marriage in name only" between her and her husband.

It was so sad for me to see that happen in the life of those pastor's wives. It seemed they had sacrificed so much in the ministry only to experience a miserable life that ended in a failed marriage.

If there is anything I can thank the Lord for in my early marriage and ministry, it is that He spotlighted those negative things and made them so vivid in my heart and mind that I actually began to reverse any sign of possible failure before its conception.

Now, let me give you some positive things that I learned and implemented.

1. I saw the need to continue to date my husband, so we tried to go out on a date at least once a week. We did not have a lot of money, but it does not take money to date. You and your husband must find time together away from the children and ministering to other people. That was one of my greatest challenges. Your children will always have needs, especially when they are young. And it is for sure that the ministry will afford a continual stream of "needy people." So we must stay committed to what caused the marriage in the first place. It was "the date."

2. I also prayed and ask the Lord that we would not fail in our marriage. Not only that we would not divorce, but that we would have a happy life together. I asked Him that when we missed the mark, His grace would carry us and provide for us the healing and the answers needed to survive. And God was faithful.

3. I kept my priorities in tact as much as I could: God and myself, J. D, my children, and our church.

Please understand what I am saying when I put myself and the Lord as first priority. I had to make sure that my relationship with Him always stayed in the number one position. That meant that I had to take care of not only my communication with my heavenly Father, but also I had to take care of my mind and body so that I could fulfill all the other priorities in my life.

For it is Satan's goal to get you and me to put ourselves last when it comes to taking care of our spirit, soul, and body. The reason that he wants this to happen is so all the other priorities of our life have the potential of falling apart. Our enemy does not care how it happens or when it happens. His only concern is that we lose everything that is precious to us in life. And he first attacks the order of our life.

Now, the Lord will prompt you to care for yourself so that you can minister to Him and to your family and your church. For you and I cannot allow those things to get out of sync because when that happens, unhappiness and misery follow close behind. Then when you read the scripture in the twenty-third Psalm, where David wrote about "goodness and mercy following you all the days of your life," you begin to question the validity of those anointed words.

For it is the strategy of our enemy to cause us to begin to question the Lord's Word, just like he did with Eve. He wants you and me to believe that our Father's words are void of power and authenticity. And if he cannot get you to believe that lie, he will simply go around and tell you that God is a respecter of persons. He will let it appear that your heavenly Father is more concerned with others than with you, that your needs are down the ladder when it comes to importance. Any way that he can to deceive you and me concerning our Father, he will exhaust all his resources.

You see, with the call to the ministry comes the urgency of eternity. Inside our hearts, the call burns with the desire to win lost souls to Jesus. Now, we may deviate from that vision at one time or another because of things like tradition, programs, and even church order. But the Holy Spirit will convict us and help us to focus on the reason for which we are called.

And with that urgency of eternity residing inside us, our

spirit is able to handle the "weight" of the call and the surging pressure to fulfill our destiny as ministers of the gospel. But our minds and bodies are not in the "incorruptible state" yet. Therefore, our mind has to be renewed daily by the Word of God according to Romans 12:2. And our bodies have to have proper nourishment, exercise, and rest, for we will not put on incorruption until the resurrection.

Now, our spirit receives eternal life and lays down eternal death at the "new birth." But our mind and body are still susceptible to death. So we have to follow certain physical laws in order for our minds and bodies to stay in tact long enough to allow God's plan in our life to succeed. And that is His plan for you, precious pastor's wife. He has put forth His kingdom in your life so that you will succeed.

So, if you are a young pastor's wife, learn this lesson now. Put your relationship with the Lord first. And with that, take care of your mind and body so that you can focus on your husband, your children and family, and then your ministry.

If you are no longer a young woman with the vim and vigor of youth, it is never too late to get your priorities in order. Just this one statement that Jesus made to His disciples concerning the rich young ruler being saved gives you and me the assurance that God can do anything, anytime. It says in Matthew 19:26, "But Jesus beheld them, and said unto them, with men this is impossible; but with God all things are possible."

It is interesting to note that Matthew wrote that Jesus "beheld them." That means He fixed his eyes intently on the disciples so they could focus on His words of truth. And then He used the words "all things" in the description of what was possible as far as God was concerned. And the words "all things" simply means "all things." He said that impossibilities lie in the hands of you and me, but not in Him. And if you will notice, the Lord did not give the condition of years or age in reference to the possibilities that were afforded us through Him.

So, set your heart upon Him and make Him first in your life. Allow the Lord to "keep" your marriage. For He is the one who keeps us in every aspect of our lives, and that includes our marriage.

OVER FIFTY AND JOYFULLY HAPPY

I am a product of that "keeping." His Word says in 2 Thessalonians 3:3, "But the Lord is faithful, who shall stablish you, and keep you from evil." It matters not how many times we may read a certain portion of Scripture; until the Holy Spirit brings the revelation of His Word into our heart, it sometimes seems either nonapplicable or too far-reaching in our faith to believe it was written for us.

Concerning this particular verse, I had read it many times. I even studied the Greek word meanings so that I might understand exactly what the Holy Spirit was trying to get across. And I learned that He is *faithful*, which means that He is completely trustworthy and reliable to produce what He says He will. What I love about the Lord is that He first tells us who He is and what He is capable of doing before He gives the promise of victory.

His promise, then, was that He would "stablish" us and "keep us from evil." The King James *stablish* translated from the Greek, according to *Strong's Concordance*, means "to steadfastly set; to confirm with strength; to turn resolutely in a certain direction."

Can I tell you that when I was going through trouble, the enemy would do all that He could to hide God as being a faithful God and that He was keeping me stable and protected from evil? All I could see was the trouble, pain, and grief

198

associated with the ministry, and it was trying to destroy me, my marriage, my family, and my life. I thought, sometimes, that evil was my constant companion, and it had me by the throat ready to end my life.

But God was faithful! His faithfulness was not determined by my feelings or what I was seeing and experiencing. I just had to take His Word by faith and trust Him. And I could not trust Him unless I knew Him intimately and knew His ways. I had to know, by His Spirit, how He reacted in certain situations. It was not that He was limited in my finite list of determined ways, but that when He would react or speak, I would know that it was He!

When you and I have been in marriage for any length of time, we have been afforded the choice of growing in trusting the faithfulness of God. Being married to a pastor or a minister requires a solidified trust in the faithfulness of God. We have to plug up any gaps or holes in our spirit that would deny the faithfulness of our heavenly Father.

Probably like me, you have been in situations in the ministry where you felt as though there was no alternative except to trust God to be faithful. Whether you realized it or not, that was one of the heights of your Christian life.

As for me, I trusted the faithfulness of God when it came to my marriage. I chose His principles of marriage. The Lord said that if I would "submit to my own husband," I would reap the rewards of that obedience. The word *submit* does not mean "become a doormat and be stepped upon." It means "to arrange under; to be flexible; to cooperate voluntarily, without force" (Thayer's).

I love the little homily that my husband gives at almost every wedding that he performs. It is found in Ephesians 5:22-25. Paul wrote to the church at Ephesus and to us:

> Wives, submit yourselves unto your own husbands, as
> unto the Lord. For the husband is the head of the wife,
> even as Christ is the head of the church: and he is the
> savior of the body. Therefore as the church is subject
> unto Christ, so let the wives be to their own husbands in
> every thing. Husbands, love your wives, even as Christ
> also loved the church, and gave himself for it.
>
> —Ephesians 5:22–23

J. D. uses the word *obey* in the wedding ceremony for the vow of the wife to the husband. There never fails to be a small sound of laughter or an obvious grin when the bride repeats the word *obey*. He then proceeds to tell the bride and groom, along with the congregation, what the word *obey* means in this vow.

He then moves to the groom and gives him the instruction of his role as the bride's husband. He is to love her like Christ loves the church. How did Christ love the church? Well, Jesus never did anything for himself; it was always for His church. He loved His church unconditionally and unselfishly. He gave His life for the church.

J. D. instructs the groom that he is to love his bride in that manner—that when he goes to work, he goes to work for his bride. When he buys a house or he buys any necessity, he buys them for his bride. The groom is to treat his bride like that precious vessel of fine china that is fragile and so valuable to him. Everything that he does is done for her. Then you can ask, "What bride would not want to cooperate with that kind of love?"

The only thing to remember in the instruction that Paul gives to us is that we cannot be responsible for our spouse's duty as the husband and priest of the home. If he is not responding the way that we think he should respond, we have no right to alter our responsibility as his wife. Our obligation in the obedience of submission rests with the Lord. We submit to our own husbands without demanding certain responses from them. Our responsibility comes absent of any demands from him. In other words, we take care of our own business.

The happiness and fulfillment of a "marriage made in heaven" comes in our obedience to submission. Granted, when both the husband and wife have taken the principles of a godly marriage and applied them in their lives, there will be great joy and happiness. But rest assured, misery will be your partner either if you try to make your spouse adhere to his duty or you show resentment toward him because you are following your obligation, but he is not. That is called selfishness.

After thirty-four years of marriage and learning some of these principles the hard way, I have realized and experienced a wonderful, happy marriage with my sweetheart, J. D.

We have both made mistakes at times in the application of God's principles. But we have never stopped loving, caring, and striving for a godly marriage together.

Our determination was to start happy and end happy. And by the grace and mercy and faithfulness of God, He has caused that to happen. Our love for each other is deeper than we ever could have imagined. All the trials, misunderstandings, pain, and suffering we have endured as a couple did not separate us from God's love or each other. We had determined to be happy in life.

We knew that there may come a time in our life when the children would leave home and maybe there would be no place to pastor. Maybe because of health or other unforeseen circumstances, we were left with only each other. And we had determined not only to love each other, but to like each other and live happily together. It always boils down to *choice*.

So, choose to be happy. Trust the Lord with your marriage. Ask His help in walking in His principles, and make the choice to live without bitterness and unforgiveness. His joy will always be your strength, and He will pronounce "blessing" upon you and your husband. And growing old with the shepherd will be the greatest time in being married to the shepherd!

God bless you, precious pastor's wife!

For additional copies of this book or other Christian resources, contact us at:

Life Worth Living Ministries
1324 Seven Springs Blvd.
Box 333
New Port Richey, FL 34655
www.lifeworthliving.cc